# Meanii

*Coaching with Meaning and Spirituality* aims to help coaches with those occasions where a client's search for meaning needs to be addressed and explored. Working with spirituality in a coaching context can be difficult and unfamiliar for coaches, but in this book Peter Hyson provides a vocabulary to facilitate this exploration, and ultimately to help coaches to address their clients' doubts and worries, especially in an economic climate where old certainties may be lost.

Part One of this text argues the case for why coaches should be willing and able to explore areas of meaning and spirituality with coachees. It provides definitions and terminology. Part Two uses case studies and activities to help coaches apply these definitions to specific contexts that we might face as coaches. The final part provides some deeper skill development and extended resources.

This book looks at motivation; legacy; drive to succeed; increasing profit; maintaining work-life balance; stress, breakdown and crises; and qualities of effective leadership. It will be especially useful for professional coaches, both the experienced and the relatively new, who coach in a variety of contexts. It aims to stimulate a new area of discussion across the wider coaching profession.

**Peter Hyson** has followed careers ranging from swimming coach and teacher to TV producer and business coach. He has a Master's degree in Leadership Development and Managing Change and professional membership of the Association for Coaching and the European Mentoring and Coaching Council. Hyson has worked with senior leaders in the City, charities and voluntary sectors, and is also a member of the Professional Speaking Association.

# Essential Coaching Skills and Knowledge
Series Editors: Gladeana McMahon,
Stephen Palmer and Averil Leimon

The **Essential Coaching Skills and Knowledge** series provides an accessible and lively introduction to key areas in the developing field of coaching. Each title in the series is written by leading coaches with extensive experience and has a strong practical emphasis, including illustrative vignettes, summary boxes, exercises and activities. Assuming no prior knowledge, these books will appeal to professionals in business, management, human resources, psychology, counselling and psychotherapy, as well as students and tutors of coaching and coaching psychology.

www.routledgementalhealth.com/essential-coaching-skills

*Titles in the series:*

**Essential Business Coaching**
*Averil Leimon, François Moscovici and Gladeana McMahon*

**Achieving Excellence in Your Coaching Practice:
How to Run a Highly Successful Coaching Business**
*Gladeana McMahon, Stephen Palmer and Christine Wilding*

**A Guide to Coaching and Mental Health: The Recognition and Management of Psychological Issues**
*Andrew Buckley and Carole Buckley*

**Essential Life Coaching Skills**
*Angela Dunbar*

**101 Coaching Strategies**
*Edited by Gladeana McMahon and Anne Archer*

**Group and Team Coaching**
*Christine Thornton*

**Coaching Women to Lead**
*Averil Leimon, François Moscovici and Helen Goodier*

**Developmental Coaching: Life Transitions and Generational Perspectives**
*Edited by Stephen Palmer and Sheila Panchal*

**Cognitive Behavioural Coaching in Practice:
An Evidence Based Approach**
*Edited by Michael Neenan and Stephen Palmer*

**Brief Coaching: A Solution Focused Approach**
*Chris Iveson, Evan George and Harvey Ratner*

**Interactional Coaching**
*Michael Harvey*

**Solution Focused Coaching in Practice**
*Bill O'Connell, Stephen Palmer and Helen Williams*

**Coaching with Meaning and Spirituality**
*Peter Hyson*

# Coaching with Meaning and Spirituality

*Peter Hyson*

LONDON AND NEW YORK

First published 2013
by Routledge
27 Church Road, Hove, East Sussex BN3 2FA

Simultaneously published in the USA and Canada
by Routledge
711 Third Avenue, New York, NY 10017

*Routledge is an imprint of the Taylor & Francis Group, an informa business*

© 2013 Peter Hyson

The right of Peter Hyson to be identified as author of this work has been asserted by him in accordance with sections 77 and 78 of the Copyright, Designs and Patents Act 1988.

All rights reserved. No part of this book may be reprinted or reproduced or utilised in any form or by any electronic, mechanical, or other means, now known or hereafter invented, including photocopying and recording, or in any information storage or retrieval system, without permission in writing from the publishers.

*Trademark notice*: Product or corporate names may be trademarks or registered trademarks, and are used only for identification and explanation without intent to infringe.

*British Library Cataloguing in Publication Data*
A catalogue record for this book is available from the British Library

*Library of Congress Cataloging in Publication Data*
Hyson, Peter
  Coaching with meaning and spirituality/Peter Hyson.
      pages cm. – (Essential coaching skills and knowledge)
    Includes bibliographical references and index.
  1. Personal coaching. I. Title.
  BF637.P36H97 2013
  158.3–dc23                                   2012030416

ISBN: 978–0–415–59745–6 (hbk)
ISBN: 978–0–415–59746–3 (pbk)
ISBN: 978–0203–0–6931–8 (ebk)

Typeset in New Century Schoolbook
by Swales & Willis Ltd, Exeter, Devon

Printed and bound by CPI Group (UK) Ltd, Croydon, CR0 4YY

# Dedication

To Hilary, who inspires me in ways too numerous to list.

# Contents

*Preface* xiii
*Acknowledgements* xv

## Part One: Setting the scene 1

### 1 What's missing? 3
Overview 3
The quest for meaning 3
Why is there a need for this book? 4
A word about language 6
What is 'coaching'? 7
The development of coaching and the
search for meaning 8
What's missing and where next? 9
So what? 13

### 2 Meaning and spirituality 15
Overview 15
Part 1: The changing context 16
Part 2: Meaning and sense-making 23
Part 3: Spirituality 37
Summary 46
Part 4: Further activities 46

## Part Two: Putting into practice — 49

### 3 Spirituality and work-life balance — 51
Overview — 51
Part 1: Work–life balance — 52
Part 2: The search for meaning — 60
Part 3: The expression of spirituality — 66
Summary — 75
Part 4: Further activities — 76

### 4 Spirituality and crises — 83
Overview — 83
Part 1: Crises — 86
Part 2: The coaching implications — 88
Part 3: The coach as alchemist — 94
Part 4: Rituals — 98

### 5 Spirituality and business — 101
Overview — 101
Part 1: Is work a suitable context? — 102
Part 2: Overcoming barriers — 115
Part 3: The characteristics of spiritually intelligent business leaders — 128
Part 4: Further activities — 133

## Part Three: Skills and resources — 139

### 6 Developing the coach's skills — 141
Overview — 141
Introduction — 142
Spirituality — 143
Coaching skills — 152
Language skills — 159
Listening skills — 164
Question skills — 165
Professional practice — 172
Postscript — 175

| | | |
|---|---|---|
| **7** | **Additional resources** | **177** |
| | Overview | 177 |
| | In-depth articles | 177 |
| | Further resources | 197 |
| | Biography of a Cheshire Cat: Why me? | 199 |
| | *Notes* | 203 |
| | *Bibliography* | 211 |
| | *Index* | 217 |

# Preface

I was prompted to write this book because of growing research on Emotional Intelligence and the importance of finding meaning. This research has also highlighted a further 'intelligence': Spiritual Intelligence. But the application of this in the coaching (and indeed wider business) context is still hampered by twin concerns, first about the validity of even raising ideas of meaning and spirituality in the work context, and second by the lack of a common vocabulary and concept-framework.

A well-known poem by Robert Frost (Frost, 1916) talks about the road less travelled. The theme of this book is not the only 'road' for coaching. But it *is* a road less travelled. And my argument is that for many of our clients it is a road that may indeed 'make all the difference'. As I write this book, various parts of the world are struggling with recession. Parts of our financial institutions are in deep trouble and shockwaves reverberate across the world; pundits aplenty are seeking to analyse, diagnose and treat, to asking questions of meaning, of being, of spirit. This just might prove to be a timely book. My starting point is: if they *could* be right, what are the implications for our coaching practice? Why is it a road less travelled?

This is essentially a practical book. It is *not* a book that necessarily needs to be followed avidly and progressively from front to back. You will not find lots of coaching models reproduced here, though I will point you in the direction of where to find them should you wish to learn more. As such, I have selected a few models on the basis that they fit particularly well with my subject matter. I am not claiming they are the only models or indeed intrinsically the best models. I am merely using them as hooks upon which to hang the specific concepts of 'meaning' and 'spirituality'.

It is a book especially but not exclusively for professional coaches, both the experienced and the relatively new, who coach in a variety of contexts. It hopes to stimulate a discussion across the wider coaching profession.

## The book in a nutshell

This book falls into three parts. Part One, 'Setting the scene', argues the case for why all of us as coaches should be willing and able to explore areas of meaning and spirituality to see if these are relevant to our coachees. It provides some definitions and terminology to attune our ears. Part Two, 'Putting into practice', applies these definitions to specific contexts that we might face as coaches and uses case studies and activities to give coaches both skill and confidence to apply them. Part Three, 'Skills and resources', provides some deeper skill-development and extended resources.

# Acknowledgements

As always, many people have contributed to the formation of this book. And as always the responsibility for what has translated onto the written page is mine. Most importantly, thanks go to my colleague Chris Howley. His diligence in commenting on the emerging versions, his academic and training skills, his creative thinking and especially his unfailing encouragement has been exceptional. My thanks also to those who allowed me to use their stories as a basis for the Case Studies, for their honesty, insights and graciousness.

Equally, my family deserve thanks – freely and gratefully given – for tolerance in times when I've been mentally absent in planning and reflection and for countless discussions over meal tables and the like.

Especially my thanks go to those who have coached me, those who have been coaches alongside me and those who have allowed me the privilege of coaching them. They keep my mind alive to new possibilities and ideas.

I still believe that coaching is one of the most formative and transformational learning opportunities and if this book prompts some further thought and exploration it will have more than served its purpose.

# Part One

## Setting the scene

# 1

# What's missing?

**Overview**

This chapter argues a need for this book because the topics of meaning and spirituality are now being discussed more openly and widely and coachees are increasingly likely to be wrestling with them. Yet there are few if any books that relate them into coaching and coaching skills. It then provides definitions of *spirituality* and *coaching* and argues that the value gained from them makes it essential.

**The quest for meaning**

The quest for meaning, the feeling of being drawn by and to something external and the drive to contribute back alongside what we take out, seems to be universal. It can be present in people not necessary regarded as 'spiritual' or indeed even particularly humanitarian. For example:

> This is the true joy in life, the being used for a purpose recognised by yourself as a mighty one ... I am of the opinion that my life belongs to the whole community, and as long as I live it is my privilege to do for it whatever I can.

These words were penned by George Bernard Shaw, renowned as a playwright rather than a spiritual philosopher. Yet they contain much of the essence of what spirituality is about.

One of our roles as coaches is to help our coachees recognise those things that, like the political prisoner, they are

## Box 1.1

Two former political prisoners met up again many years later. One was now a successful businessman with all the trappings of success. The other was shabbily dressed, grubby and bitter. 'It's all very well for you,' he moaned, 'you've always had all the advantages. Even when we were doing forced labour you would always carry much heavier loads than me. I nearly broke my back and I still couldn't keep up. You know how often the guards beat me for it.'

For over an hour the businessman listened to a torrent of anger and recriminations for the injustices of life. When his companion finally ran out of invectives he turned to him and said, 'My friend there is only one difference between us. I put the loads down when I left the prison. Why are you still carrying them?'

still carrying. Not, of course, in the realm of counselling or therapy, but in the realms of unchallenged assumptions, preconceived restrictions, of blinkers, if you will. The story of the two former prisoners raises a triple-challenge: at one level, it's a challenge about *what* we continue to needlessly carry long after the event; at another level, it's a challenge about *why* we continue to carry them; and at a third, deeper level, it's a challenge about what underlying *needs* they reveal.

## Why is there a need for this book?

First, it provides practical activities for an area rising in significance, that of meaning and spirituality. Issues such as climate change and economic downturn have forced more people to think and be aware of our individual and corporate place within a global web of interconnectedness. John Donne put it rather more graphically:

> No man is an island, entire of itself; every man is a piece of the continent, a part of the main. If a clod be washed away by the sea, Europe is the less: . . . any man's death diminishes me, because I am involved in mankind.[1]

Second, coaches are increasingly likely to encounter people engaging with these ideas, however subconsciously. And since the coach's role is to offer clients the opportunity and support to achieve their full potential, we need to be in the forefront of such an exploration. This book will enable coaches to identify when the questions may be emerging.

Third, there is an urgent need for some clear, agreed language, definitions, concepts, models and coaching skills in order to explore these things. This book aims to contribute to an ongoing debate by its use of story, image and metaphor: not only because these are effective communication tools but also because metaphors creatively challenge our thinking, help us move outside previous assumptions and engage our right-brain in a world dominated by left-brain. Some key points will appear in more than one chapter but they are important precursors for understanding that chapter for those who may not have read the previous chapter; they also serve as a reminder for those who have.

### Box 1.2

In 1512 a violent and aggressive young warrior named Inigo was severely injured defending Pamplona. Invalided home, he spent many happy hours dreaming of the brave deeds he would perform when recovered and the beautiful maiden who would swoon at his feet. But over time he began to tire of these great deeds. There was little to read in the castle where he lay so he had to make do with religious texts about Jesus Christ and about the early Saints. But he soon began to imagine himself outdoing the austerity and piety of the saints! For many hours he alternated between dreams of war and dreams of devotion. But then he noticed something more: whilst at the time each type of dream was equally satisfying, shortly after the dreams of heroics and maidenly virtue ended he felt listless and unsatisfied, whereas with those of outdoing the saints, he felt excited and challenged. After further reflection, he began to recognise the former as characterised by a destructive inner mood and the latter by a creative mood. He began to spend

> more time with the creative inner mood, from which emerged Simple Contemplation and Spiritual Exercises. The man was St Ignatius of Loyola; the result was the Ignation Spiritual Exercises.

Point 1: *Spiritual reflection can challenge and encourage creativity, becoming deeply satisfying.*

One of the challenges for professional coaches (or any other professional) is to maintain creativity and development, to keep taking our skills to new breadths and depths. This is not about blindly following any fad, trend or gimmick; it's about critically examining emerging trends to test relevance and applicability. Sometimes that reveals entirely new areas; sometimes it challenges preconceptions and prejudices; sometimes it reveals a blind alley. So what follows invites critical reflection, experimentation and experience.

## A word about language

This topic is explored in more depth in Chapter 2. Here, I introduce some core terminology that might begin to move us forward. Let me be clear at the outset (and repeat with frequency): spirituality is *not* the same as religion. It is perfectly possible to have spirituality without religion – though arguably more difficult to have religion without spirituality. At the risk of initially over-simplifying in the cause of brevity: *spirituality* is 'an innate need to connect to something larger than ourselves';[2] *religion* is *one* of the ways that people may express that externally and organisationally.

Any terminology – and language itself – is symbolic, representational and prone to confuse. There is usually more lying behind it than is conveyed by it. In the context here, I want to distinguish between two types of terminology.

*Gateway terminology* is the hint to bring out the detective in us, the clues that something else may be going on under the surface. Like the best forensic clues, they can easily be overlooked by the 'untrained' eye but if pursued can reveal all sorts of leads towards discovering the broader picture. Gateway terms in the context of meaning and spirituality might include: 'give back'; 'something missing'; 'fulfilment'; 'purpose'.

*Core terminology* is perhaps more akin to the threads of a tapestry: a very clear and inherent part of a broader picture. Revealing the whole picture often requires some unravelling (if I might use that in the metaphor of a tapestry). Core terms might include: 'spirit'; 'meaning'; 'greater good'; 'Higher Purpose'.

To place this in the coaching context, gateway terminology may often be an aside, a throwaway remark, added in parenthesis to the subject matter currently taking place. The skill required from the coach is first to spot it at all and then to craft the questions that will explore with the coachee exactly how significant it is. Very often the coachee is not yet conscious of what is bubbling away under the surface. The significance of the throwaway remark is often missed by the person uttering it as well as those hearing it. But spot the clues, pursue the trail, and a rich potential may emerge. The coachee of course has every right to decline this opportunity for whatever reason.

Point 2: *Gateway terminology is often the most fruitful area to explore because it is bubbling away below the surface but has not yet been consciously articulated.*

Core terminology is much clearer. Here, the coachee is already aware of the language they're using and its implications, has chosen to do so deliberately and is willing, even keen, to pursue what that means in practice.

More of this in Chapter 2.

## What is 'coaching'?

There are almost as many definitions as there are coaches and academics. In this book *coaching* refers to those situations where the coach may have little or no direct experience in the working context of the coachee but skilfully uses a series of questions to prompt the thinking and emerging understanding of the coachee so that they are themselves able to identify, own and implement the courses of action. (This differs from *mentoring*, where the mentor has at least a working knowledge of context and a remit that includes both knowledge-sharing and door-opening.) Within coaching, I have used *executive coaching* as equating with *business coaching*: and consisting of regular meetings skilfully conducted to bring about positive changes in business behaviour in a limited time frame.[3] *Life coaching* is the appropriation of similar skills and techniques but usually begins and predominantly continues to operate outside the work context.

In practice there are overlaps and untidy edges between and across each of these areas.

## The development of coaching and the search for meaning

The year 2009 marked the 50th anniversary of the publication of Viktor Frankl's book *Man's Search for Meaning* (under a different title). The search itself of course goes back much further, even to the speculative cave drawings of our oldest ancestors. It has been more obvious in some professions such as teaching or nursing, missionary or pioneer – the 'vocations'. Philosophers also travelled in the realm of 'meaning', as did some of the greatest scientists. (Einstein is reputed to have formulated much of his thinking about relativity while gazing meditatively at dust particles in a shaft of sunlight streaming through his window.) But for most people, it remained the unknown, unvisited and rather scary domain graphically etched by the early map-writers: 'There be dragons'. Their search for meaning, at least in the West, was gleaned from the great institutions: the universities, the Government and the Church.

The opposite of *meaning* was commonly assumed to be *unknown*. Therefore, the more things that were explained, the more the realm in which to explore the search for meaning was assumed to shrink. Yet discovering *knowledge* does not equate with discovering *meaning*. The explosion of knowledge certainly hasn't diminished the appetite for finding meaning. So where now might the search be conducted?

Even those great institutions of the State (in the UK, Parliament, the Church, even the BBC) have been eroded of their credibility. In parallel the sense of stability has been dented by the collapse of jobs for life, of unfettered and infinitely expanding wealth. But while the outward expressions may have crumbled, the inner hunger for *meaning* remains and must seek satisfaction.

In recent decades, the temptation was to fill the void with materialism. Materialism brought many of the same rewards and satisfaction. But it didn't necessarily bring a sense of meaning. For some, the hollowness of materialism became the backcloth for a more profound questioning and a return to a search for meaning, fulfilment and balance. Most generations are conducting this search, though its context and terminology is often different – as we'll see later. But rarely is that expressed within the context of paid employment.

In the year of the new millennium, C. Michael Thompson noted:

> those who discuss the economics of work seldom deal adequately with issues of meaning . . . And those who deal with the meaning of life seldom appear competent to deal with the economics of work.[4]

There is a need. It is rarely even acknowledged, never mind met. It may just be that the current economic downturn and the debates thus engendered about bonuses, responsibility and the search for meaning has provided the bush-fire that burns away the deep undergrowth, thus allowing long-forgotten seeds to break through and flourish again in the scorched earth.

## What's missing and where next?

There are some signs that we may be, as Shakespeare described it in *Julius Caesar*, 'in a full sea', a flood, at this point in time. Even before the banking crisis refocused our attention on a broader sense of function and purpose, The Chartered Institute of Personnel and Development (CIPD) *Employee Attitudes and Engagement Survey 2006* noted that 52 per cent of the 2,000 respondents said their work was 'meaningful' to them. A recent article, simply entitled

'Generation Why',[5] outlined a survey of more than 1,000 coaches with 82 per cent stating they dealt with meaning and purpose in their work and three-quarters said it was becoming more prevalent. 'There is a tide in the affairs of men' (*Julius Caesar*, Act 4, Sc. 3).

One of the features of being in a flood is that old familiar landmarks are lost. There can be a sense of powerlessness, of uncertainty, even fear. Our priorities are refocused and we challenge previous assumptions. In other words, we seek a new meaning. The opening of the floodgates is often triggered by a crisis.[6] Those facing massive change through divorce or redundancy are, not surprisingly, most willing to explore issues of meaning. Those facing age-related change also visit the search for meaning, though how that is expressed differs generationally: baby-boomers (those now 50+) often express it in terms of legacy, those from Generation X (30–45 year-olds) tend to wrestle with 'Is this all there is?', while Generation Y (the under 30s) wrestle with how to reconcile their expectations of a perfect work-life balance with the reality they experience.

> **Activity**
>
> Print out the quotation from George Bernard Shaw at the beginning of this chapter and give it to a coachee (preferably unsourced). Ask them to comment on what thoughts and feelings it prompts in them.

As people have experienced the impact of effective coaching on their performance at *work* they are more open than ever to seeing coaching as a significant part of their life *outside* work, as a proactive way of dealing with the everyday issues of living in an ever-changing environment and of their personal search for meaning and even spirituality. It is part of the argument of this book that we really are at that 'tide in the affairs of men' and that it is a significant responsibility of coaches to help clients to recognise those things that, 'taken at the flood, lead on to fortune' but if 'omitted, all the voyage of their life/Is bound in shallows and in miseries'.

I am not suggesting that questions of *meaning* are the same as questions of *spirituality*: it is perfectly possible to ask questions about meaning out of an intellectual need to understand; it is possible to ask them from a secular emotional empathy and desire to help others. But sometimes within the search there is the vaguest feeling that there might be 'something more out there'.

This book will argue that this search is universal and as such is ignored or underdeveloped at our peril (rather like our physical, emotional or intellectual development). Spirituality becomes a distinct intelligence – SQ. It takes its place as one tool in the coach's toolkit, alongside an understanding of adult development, personality types, values, etc.

Sir John Whitmore describes this area as the 'transpersonal' (literally beyond the personal, recognising the interconnectedness of individuals, families, communities, organisations and life itself): 'It recognizes and works with the yearning ingrained in the human psyche for something beyond the personal, beyond the material and the everyday that is often described as the spiritual.'[7] Significantly, Whitmore makes the point that the transpersonal is a progression on from the search for meaning, a continuum that moves into the spiritual.

### Activity

Who do you consider to be spiritual leaders? They don't necessarily need to be well known; they might even be fictional. They don't necessarily need to be considered leaders in spirituality. When you've got enough names, write down a general list of the gifts or things that you admire in them, what it is that prompts you to label them as 'spiritual'. What do you notice?

Some commonly identified traits are listed in Chapter 7.

SETTING THE SCENE

Most coaches I've spoken to say they have rarely or never been into the realm of the spiritual with their coachees. These people are excellent coaches, highly experienced, very skilled and empathic listeners.

So what's happening? Is it mistaken to argue that the search for meaning and spirituality is an inherent part of becoming fully human? Or might it be that we're simply missing the clues and cues?

### Activity

Imagine a coaching scenario with someone who's feeling frustrated at work – Rashida. Her promotion is being blocked by a self-serving manager in an organisation unwilling to listen. It's an easily recognised situation and we may even be able to put names and faces to the players, hear their voices and their words. And even if we've not been there ourselves, we're likely to have read something similar in a book or heard it from other people – we can identify with it. This gives us the hooks on which we can begin to hang some information in order to draft some questions for Rashida. We might explore Rashida's relationships with her colleagues, how other people experience the behaviour of the self-serving manager, why she thinks the organisation doesn't want to listen, her own role in the organisation, where she'd like to get to in say five years, what she currently finds frustrating, what would need to change. Maybe there are issues around gender, diversity, etc.

*But* . . . what if this is the wrong hook? What if there's something deeper going on in Rashida? What if we delve into the iceberg deep beneath the surface, progressing from actions, behaviours, beliefs and values to what makes Rashida fundamentally Rashida? Here we enter the murky hinterland between coaching and counselling and I really am *not* advocating transgressing that boundary. We enter looking for different things . . . So suppose that after Rashida has told us her story, at the point where a confident relationship has been formed, instead of asking the business-based questions, what if we were to ask her a potentially surprising question: 'What might set your spirit free?' We'll come back to Rashida and her response and how the coaching might progress in Chapter 6.

Generally coaches rightly try to avoid giving advice or steer or influence. In reality, we can rarely be totally objective and non-influencing (and arguably shouldn't be anyway). In this area of exploring meaning and spirituality, because of its unfamiliarity as the 'road less travelled', the coach may need to take more of a lead, to be companion.

> **Box 1.3**
>
> Some years ago I was being guided around the newly post-communist Prague with a companion who had worked in the country for a number of years. One afternoon we found ourselves in a part of the city my companion realised she did not know and where she didn't feel qualified to guide. That posed a dilemma: did we go back to find a place more familiar to my companion, or risk a journey into the unknown? Initially it was quite a difficult choice: Prague was still quite an uncertain place to be. But eventually we broke new ground. And by doing so, in a remote side street we discovered the house of author Franz Kafka – which prompted me to re-visit his writings and renew my fascination with them. The value of the journey lay not in the knowledge of the guide but her willingness to accompany me into the unknown.

## So what?

This is a fundamental question: is there actually any real *benefit* from all this? After all, I may be correct in my contention that spirituality is *missing* – but does it *matter*?! My contention is that it is a necessary prerequisite for wholeness, for both the individual and for the organisation, and that the domain of the spirit adds real value:

- for the coach: at the very least as an additional, valuable and versatile tool for the toolkit;
- for the coachee: presenting opportunities for significant personal development in an area that can significantly impact business and broader life;

- for the organisation: research suggests those who find meaning in their work and in themselves appear to be more committed, more competent and more effective both with the business and with their colleagues. And it appears to be contagious.

There's a further point here. We as coaches are not blank sheets or perfect vessels: we have our own hurts, dislikes and blind spots. In the same way that before choosing to enter the realm of business coaching we need to resolve any of our outstanding issues about money, power, multinational corporations and the like, so we need to resolve any potential blind spots we might have towards spirituality or – perhaps more likely – religion. If our strong support or opposition is likely to colour our responses, then we should back away and call in someone more suitable to that client's needs. Tough to do – but a professional necessity.

The premise of this book is straightforward: we are inherently spiritual beings; this is an essential part of our makeup and necessary for our completeness. However, spirituality is readily confused with religion and hence avoided as the final taboo. Even if the subject crops up, as it does with increasing frequency, there is still a common assumption that it should not enter work. Yet to avoid it is to leave individuals incomplete and organisations less than they might be. This book provides some background material on the subject matter, suggests a common vocabulary and provides numerous exercises to help coaches explore with a little more confidence and competence.

Point 3: *These questions of meaning and spirituality are already being asked, they are fundamental to human development and add value to both the individual and the organisation.*

# 2

# Meaning and spirituality

## Overview

Chapter 1 introduced the concept of *spirituality*, defined it as 'an innate need to connect to something larger than ourselves' and looked at what makes it distinct from religion. It then considered different types of coaching and why coaching has grown exponentially over the past few decades as business needs have overlapped with personal development awareness. I argued that the quest for spirituality is a universal one and suggested several reasons why, in the West at least, it is often a road less travelled – including an unchallenged assumption that it is somehow inappropriate in the workplace and a lack of familiar terminology.

This chapter covers three things. Part 1 looks at *the changing context* and asks whether we're caught up in *mythic entrancement*; it assesses the importance of *noble goals* and of *values, beliefs, religion* and *spirituality*. Part 2 concentrates on *meaning* and *sense-making*; it explores meaning and the transpersonal; it also introduces the ongoing case study of David and uses a coaching session to examine how often meaning-based terminology is used, often unconsciously and unnoticed, starts to identify some trends and then provides some activities to help coaches apply this to their own practice. Part 3 concentrates on *spirituality*; it introduces a preliminary definition and considers emerging research about *Spiritual Intelligence*. Part 4 contains activities to help coaches put these ideas into practice.

## Part 1: The changing context

Over the past few years of economic turmoil, people are increasingly realising that their *job* is their real source of financial stability: that they have to live within the means of their *income* not within the means of their *assets*.[1] This is also true for those whose income is from social security benefits payments. At the same time, Dick Bolles' 1970 book about finding out who you are as a person and where you find meaning in life – *What Color Is Your Parachute?*[2] – has returned to the bestseller lists. Meanwhile a plethora of magazine articles, news reports and financial advisors warn of the need to rethink traditional assumptions about retirement age, leisure, satisfaction, etc. Around 10 years ago, *The Management Report* (McCartney and Holby, 2003) found that:

- nearly three-quarters of workers were interested in learning to live the spiritual side of their values;
- 40 per cent of UK managers would value the opportunity to discuss workplace spirituality with their colleagues;
- 53 per cent are already experiencing tensions between the spiritual side of their values and their work.

Something is afoot.

In order to provide the best possible development for coachees, coaches need to be aware of and critically assess the significance of these emerging trends and patterns and then become skilled in assisting coachees to articulate what they themselves may only dimly sense. Coaches must be careful not to put words into their mouths or ideas into their heads; we must be scrupulous in not transferring our agenda onto them. Good coaches are already careful about this as a matter of course.

### *Mythic entrancement*

A renewed seeking after meaning has been one of the emerging trends of recent years. Many people today are seeking after what is best for themselves and their lives. But many do not yet have the perspective to fully recognise it or the vocabulary to articulate it. This is as true for coaches as it is for coachees. It is as though we live in a trance, an hermetically-sealed box rather like the film *The Truman Show* (1998).[3] South American tribes call it *mythic entrancement* – people unable to recognise and therefore challenge or go beyond the assumptions and foundations upon which their myth, their worldview, is based. Plato gave a graphic example of mythic entrancement in his allegory of The Cave (see Box 2.1).

### Box 2.1

In his philosophical treaties *The Republic*, Plato invents the story of a group of people who had spent their entire lives chained together in a cave. All they can ever see is a series of shadows flickering on the cave wall in front of them. Over a period of time, these cave dwellers ascribe characteristics and stories to the shadows to make sense of the confusing reality they see before them. Then one day one of the prisoners is freed. He ventures to the cave mouth and beyond. He meets the people, animals and objects whose forms he has previously seen only in projection on the wall. He learns that this 'reality' is vastly different and more complex than the paradigms they'd previously imagined. In his excitement, he returns to tell the others what he's discovered. But, according to Plato's story, the prisoners find his talk far too disconcerting and he's rejected as disruptive and mad, finally being forced to flee for his life.

Highly experienced coaches are just as prone to mythic entrancement as anyone else. Younger coaches may potentially be better placed: they do at least belong to a generation more prepared to ask and think through the big issues of life and meaning than many who have gone before.

This chapter provides a general framework to some of the key terminology to break the mythic entrancement. And it argues that to do so is crucial not only for the realms of life-coaching and personal development but also for businesses.

In case all this sounds too nebulous, check out 'Management's Grand Challenges',[4] 25 core make-or-break challenges for company development that emerged from a symposium of such luminaries as Chris Argyris, Gary Hamel, Henry Mintzberg and Peter Senge. Their first three deal-breakers are:

- Ensure that the work of management serves a higher purpose ('noble, socially significant goals').
- Fully embed the ideas of community and citizenship.
- Reconstruct management's philosophical foundations ('draw lessons from such fields as biology, political science and theology').

## *'Noble goals'*

Learning lies at the heart of coaching. And the purpose of learning is the 'noble goal' of transformation. Mezirow[5] defines this transformative learning as: 'critical self-reflection, which results in the reformulation of a "meaning perspective" to allow a more inclusive, discriminating and integrative understanding of experience.' The question of meaning is covered in more depth later in this chapter; for the moment, let me simply say this book will argue that this reformulation of a meaning perspective raises questions that are potentially life changing and truly transformative. However, part of the current western mythic entrancement is a heavy emphasis on knowledge, science, understanding and intellect; often examination of a 'meaning perspective' requires expression in different terminology to that with which we are perhaps currently familiar and as such risks being ignored, under-developed or under-valued. Such is the curse of mythic entrancement.

Gerard Hughes[6] sums this up when he recounts the words of a taciturn Scottish decorator anonymised simply as 'Jock' (see Box 2.2).

In Box 2.2 we have the two main issues of this chapter in a nutshell! There *are* things that we feel for which we have neither (logical) explanation nor specific language. And even if we had, they might appear so far from the usual topics of conversation we might fear 'ma mates will think ah wis kinky'!

## Box 2.2 Jock

'Ay, ah wis in Wales in the summer, ma first holiday away frae home. D'ye know whit ah found masel' doin'? Walkin' the bloody moors wi' a wee dug. Ma mates wid've thought ah wis crazy, but ah felt happy. Ah came tae cliffs by the sea and jist sat there. The sea looked affie big and ah felt very wee, but ah wis happy. Daft, isn't it? Ah cannie tell ma mates, 'cos they'd think ah wis kinky.'

Fear of what others might think is not the only hurdle to leap if we are to explore the unknown. We may fear what we may find; we may fear the consequences of what we may find (challenged views, changed assumptions); or, like Plato's cave dwellers we may be perfectly happy with how things are and have neither the emotional nor creative energy to deal with re-orientating and its ramifications. So myopia of mythic entrancement continues unchallenged and our worldview remains intact.

That worldview is closely related to what we value or have been taught to value.

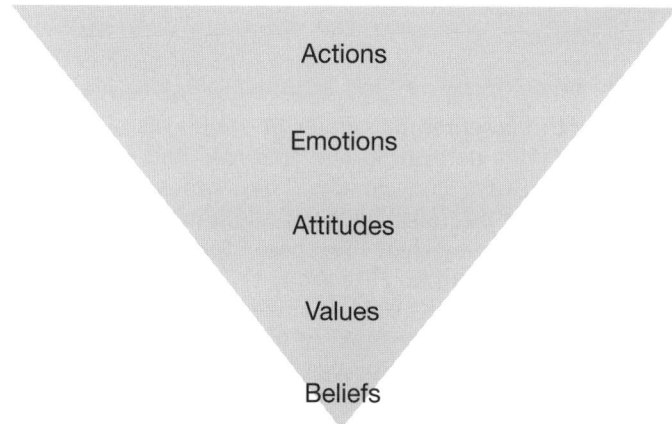

*Figure 2.1* Actions, Emotions, Attitudes, Values, Beliefs (triangle)

Our values rest on our beliefs. How we construct and link these gives us our narrative of *meaning*, of sense-making. How we put these into practice is exhibited in our attitudes, emotions and actions or behaviours.

But there's nothing new in that. It's a well-researched and well-trodden path. Freud, Jung, Maslow, Senge, Goleman, Boyatzis, all have recognised this in their work. This book takes it a stage further, moving beyond *meaning* into *spirituality*, the ultimate sense-making. Quite a 'noble path'!

And because this is a practical Handbook, this chapter includes some activities to help coaches become more familiar with recognising and using the terminology and to create some avenues to explore these issues with any coachee. It's my contention that many coachees, if not most, are in fact already asking these questions but they're often missed by both themselves and their coaches for a variety of (identifiable and avoidable) reasons. It's also my contention that, where coachees are willing to explore, they become significantly more integrated within themselves and significantly more effective in their work, thus increasing their value to themselves, to their organisations and to those around them.

But first, I have used a number of key terms without actually defining them – and hence have created a potential minefield. So at this point, let me attempt some mine clearing.

## *Values*

*Values* are the accepted principles or standards of a person or a group. They determine our attitudes and our actions, though not always consciously. They can vary not only between groups but also between the same individual at different times during their life: these I term *relative* values. But alongside these sit an elite group that I term *core* values. Core values are normally held consistently through our lives; they are what give us our sense of identity and purpose, our way of sifting between different choices, our reason for setting one direction or avoiding another. They influence the choice of people with whom we associate (or not). They may affect the type of employment we choose; and if a core value is compromised, that is likely to be a resignation issue or deal-breaker.

Over the past couple of decades, much has been written within Western societies about the differing values of the different 'generations' and especially the way they are revealed in their expectations. 'Baby-boomers', those born between the end of the Second World War and about the mid-sixties, are a good example. Their parents' values (and indeed their grandparents') were based on honesty, hard-work and ensuring family survival; they expected to remain with one company or industry throughout their working lives and expected those in return to provide (relative) security and continuity; they had no expectation of finding 'meaning' in their work. But the emerging baby-boomer generation was different, their expectations changed. They valued and expected (not merely hoped for) greater responsibility and more challenging work and to find it rewarding, both financially and in terms of satisfaction or meaning. Their values were expressed in the terminology of personal fulfilment, capped hours of work, a wider range of leisure activities and the option of change.

If those were the expectations and values of Western baby-boomers, there is a different manifestation in an upcoming generation. 'Generation Y' describes those born post-1980. The term was initially introduced to separate it from its predecessor, 'Generation X'. The first recorded use seems to be in August 1993 in the American magazine *Advertising Age*; some writers[7] use the term 'Millennium' Generation instead. The defining feature of those in Generation Y is an easy familiarity with new communications, media and digital technology and a generally more liberal approach to life. Among their values is seeking employment in organisations that demonstrate an ethical commitment, a recognition of corporate responsibility to the society in which they operate and a commitment to the well-being and wholeness of their employees. From this emerged the great clarion-cry of our age: 'work-life balance', which has earned a later chapter in its own right (see Chapter 3).

> **Activity[8]**
>
> Ask some of your coachees to identify their key values, perhaps 10–15.[9] Ask them to select the most important ones under *each* of the following headings: 'Paid work'; 'Unpaid work'; and 'Play'. Are there overlaps? Are there any values not currently being met under any of the three headings? Then ask them to identify their two or three core values – these are the ones that if transgressed at work would lead them to resign, or if transgressed by a life partner would result in them terminating the relationship.

## *Beliefs*

Beliefs generally refer to trust or truth that a statement, principle, or system is accurate and reliable, something upon which other things can reliably be built.

They are about what we hold to be true and they are one of the foundations upon which we then build our actions. Taken with our values, they are an important part defining both who and what we are.[10] At extremes, they can be self-limiting or overly optimistic. They may be positive or negative, empowering or limiting. While they may be evidentially incorrect (I may *believe* that I can fly from the top of a building, but the current weight of evidence would suggest otherwise), more often than not they have a basis in fact mixed with interpretation and applied through personal filters. They result in actions and we act as if they are true. Beliefs are therefore one of the cornerstones of coaching.

Many beliefs are formed in earliest childhood and the ensuing years may be spent carefully filtering out those things that challenge their veracity. Beliefs are our rules for life; it takes a great deal to change them and the ensuing re-alignment can be deeply difficult. (See Chapter 4 on crises.) They influence the groups to which we belong, the places we visit, the books we read, even our politics and social action. They influence how we spend our money and even whom we marry; in religion, they determine how we define 'truth' and where we place our ultimate perspective or responsibility.

Which leads me to one of the defining points of this book: the need to emphasise the crucial distinction between *religion* and *spirituality*.

## *Religion and spirituality*

*Religion* is a set of defined and agreed ritualistic beliefs and their institutional enactment. That institution commonly manages a set of agreed narratives, symbols, beliefs and practices that give meaning to their followers' experiences. These often include prayer, ritual, meditation, music and art. It tends to be both formulaic and corporate.

*Spirituality*, however, is profoundly different. In Chapter 1, I introduced Wigglesworth's definition: 'an innate need to connect with something larger than ourselves'.[11] In essence it is the opposite of formulaic and corporate. It tends to be nebulous and individual.

Point 4: *Religion is not the same as spirituality and many claim to be spiritual who would be deeply offended to be called religious.*

That is not to imply that religion is not important. But the individual does not need a religion in order to experience spirituality, even if it may sometimes be the outward manifestation of that inner spiritual experience. My assertion is that within each human lies the potential to recognise the existence of something that is greater than one's self and that has a call on us and this is what I shall henceforth refer to as *spirituality*. So Part 2 of this chapter deals more specifically with *meaning* and *sense-making*; Part 3 more specifically with *spirituality*.

## Part 2: Meaning and sense-making

One of the accusations frequently levelled at Western society and consumerism is that it knows the price of everything and the value of nothing. One result of this has been the misdirection of our innate drive to search for meaning. Yet according to Professor Martin Seligman of the Positive Psychology movement, meaning is one of the three essential requisites for happiness. (The others are pleasure and engagement). He comments that in order to live life to the full we need a sense of meaning, of belonging to and contributing to something outside ourselves. The following story, based on the Sufi tradition, illustrates this.

> **Box 2.3**
>
> A wise woman was once accused by one of her disciples of being far too out of touch with the real world. Reaching into the deepest recesses of her cloak, she produced a jewel that sparkled and shimmered in the light. She handed it over to her disciple with this task: 'Take this into the market, to the stalls that sell silverware and watch batteries and see if you can get one hundred gold coins for it.'
>
> Try as he might, however, the disciple could get no better than an offer of a handful of silver coins. He returned dejectedly to the wise woman.
>
> 'Good,' she replied. 'Now take it to a real jeweller and see what they will give you.'
>
> Ducking into the nearest such premises, the disciple was amazed to be offered many thousands of gold coins.
>
> On his return the wise woman looked deep into his eyes. 'Your understanding of real knowledge and meaning is like the stallholders'. You know the cost of everything but the value of nothing. If you seek true value and meaning, learn to be like the jeweller.'

> **Box 2.4**
>
> *Meaning* is what we draw from our experiences, the way in which we organise them and explain them in order to make sense of them – at least to our own satisfaction. Literally, it is the significance of life; the making sense of situations, from which we derive our psychological or moral sense and purpose.

The search for meaning is a realm much beloved by authors ranging from Douglas Adams[12] to Viktor Frankl[13] via Abraham Maslow,[14] Sigmund Freud[15] and countless others.

Indeed Frankl argued that the search for meaning is the primary motivation for humanity.

Objects and events do not inherently have meaning; only those that we choose to apply to them. Other people may or may not share that meaning but the meaning is the interpretation we attach in our attempt at sense-making and feeling we belong with a sense of purpose. This is true in each aspect of our life, including relationships and work.

No kind of work is inherently more or less meaningful. It depends on the attitudes that are brought to it. Most of us have met the uncaring nurse, the bullying teacher, the intrusive social worker. Equally, most of us have met the road-sweeper who takes inordinate pride in a clean and pleasant environment, the bus driver whose cheerful greeting and banter raises the smile of the passengers, etc. So while some kinds of work offer a more ready *opportunity* for finding meaning, '*all work is capable of addressing our core needs for meaning and purpose*'.[16] One of the roles of the coach, then, is to help clients explore ways in which they might find meaning and a sense of purpose.

Work offers us two opportunities to explore meaning. Initially it offers us the money for survival (what Herzberg called dissatisfaction-reduction[17]); and it provides a sense of purpose linked to self worth, achievement and security (what Herzberg called satisfaction-builders and John Haughey called the *imminent* meaning of work[18]).

*Figure 2.2* **Hertzberg; Maslow's hierarchy of needs**

There may be as many meanings or dimensions of meaning as there are people pursuing the quest. And some might be more satisfying than others! For example, in the Monty Python film *The Meaning of Life* (1983), lead-character Michael concludes the film by reading out 'the meaning of life': 'essentially, be nice to people, read a good book and don't eat fat!' In the book *The Hitchhiker's Guide to the Galaxy* the computer Deep Thought, specially built to identify the meaning of life, takes seven and a half million years to compute and check the answer before summing it up even more pithily: '42'.

My thesis is that the search for 'meaning' is intrinsically self-centred (though not necessarily self*fish*). In terms of Maslow's Hierarchy of Needs, it relates specifically to levels 3 (Belonging) and 4 (Self-esteem or Ego-Status). It is an activity of the mind. In Herzberg's terms, it relates to Level 2: Builds Satisfaction.

### Activity

*Phrase some questions for your coachees that hinge on meaning – e.g. 'What will it mean to you to achieve this goal?' 'What might give you satisfaction?' It can be useful to have these available to draw on in a coaching session if needed.*

## *Transpersonal*[19]

Transpersonal psychology studies the transpersonal, transcendent or spiritual aspects of human experience. The *Journal of Transpersonal Psychology* defines it as 'concerned with the study of humanity's highest potential, and with the recognition, understanding, and realization of unitive, spiritual, and transcendent states of consciousness' (Lajoie and Shapiro, 1992, p. 91). Transpersonal psychology therefore maintains that personal development and spiritual development are not separate boxes but stages on a continuum, irrevocably linked and equally important.

Over the past decades researchers in the area of the transpersonal include Carl Jung, William James, Abraham

Maslow and Roberto Assagioli. Sir John Whitmore maintains that 'the transpersonal is the inevitable evolution of the psychological basis of coaching'.[20]

In coaching it involves recognition of the power of the altruistic, of the desire to be of service and of the search for meaning. An article in *Management Today* notes: 'A desire to find a job with more meaning is a more common cause for exit than the pursuit of a fatter pay packet. Four out of five people say that "making the world a better place" through their work was very important or absolutely essential to them.'[21]

Clearly this is a vital area for coaches. At its best the search for transpersonal meaning can be an empowering process that helps clients discover the power and effectiveness of who they really are. It is the source of our deepest values and qualities, and ignites real strength, creativity and achievement. Untapped, it can fester away, a source of frustration and ineffectiveness.

Transpersonal coaching recognises that we have connectedness through other individuals, families, communities, societies and organisations. It reminds us that the search for meaning might be considered a journey along a pathway leading towards ultimate understanding. It asserts that the spiritual is both a valid and a valuable element of coaching.

## *Case study: David – Part one*

The following case study – fictional but based on real coaching sessions – sets the scene for what follows in the remainder of this book. Its purpose is to show how often meaning-based terminology is used in a typical coaching conversation and how responding to this terminology can significantly change the course of the ensuing coaching, leading to a deeper, wider and more effective dimension of exploration: the spiritual. It is certainly *not* intended to show perfect coaching and it may well be that you'll feel you'd do things differently or better. It's here for illustration and experimentation only. And we'll return to it and chart progress in future chapters.

## Introduction and background

David is Head of Marketing for OMG (Overseas Medical Group), a UK-based pharmaceutical company that manufactures medicines for distribution around the world. He is in his late thirties and has a respected degree in Marketing. Since he joined OMG 10 years ago he has been something of the 'rising star'; several of his projects have won awards recognising innovation in marketing and he has risen through the ranks. He was promoted to the role just over 12 months ago and joined the UK Executive Council; he would be expected to join the main board in another twelve to eighteen months. He has known the UK CEO, Morgan, ever since the latter joined the company six years previously, having been part of his induction. They get on well, respect each other's abilities and often share a drink after work, but they certainly wouldn't class themselves as close and actually know little of each other's life outside work.

His immediate boss is Sarah, the Senior Vice President for Marketing, Sales and Business Development, and one of five UK directors. She joined OMG when they took over the small business development consultancy she'd set up. She'd previously undertaken high-level consultancy for OMG, and OMG was so impressed with the work that, as they say, they 'bought the company'.

David has just returned from a six-month absence due to stress. Sarah is cautious. Amongst other things, shortly before he'd 'gone off sick', David had accused her of being hard and unfeeling (something she'd not heard before) and as a conscientious line manager, she is keen to overcome David's impression when he returns. Morale in the office is generally good but David isn't especially popular and has a reputation for being rather difficult to work with, easily flying off the handle. Over his 10 years he's built an excellent client-base (both internally and externally), being well respected for his knowledge of the business. However, in the few months before going off sick, there had been a few negative mutterings from clients – especially one internal one, Dawn, whose division is shortly to take a new drug to a market already dominated by a rival company. Sarah has suggested David works with an external coach.

## Activity

*You've been asked by Sarah to work with David and to make an initial telephone contact. At this stage, what do you see as the main issues?*

i.
ii.
iii.

1 The preliminary telephone conversation with David has now taken place and the following points have emerged:

- David had not been expecting your call, was unaware that he had been lined up for coaching and resents being made to feel a failure.
- He feels he has re-entered the workplace 'with gusto' and has already proved he's still up to the job. He's made contact with all his old clients, though he does admit surprise that several seemed rather aloof.
- He thinks that some of his fellow workers are treating him with kid-gloves, trying to over-protect him and he resents this.

At this stage:

1. *What do you consider might be the main challenges or blind spots that David faces:*

   a) *in himself?*

   i.
   ii.
   iii.
   iv.

   b) *from others?*

   i.
   ii.
   iii.
   iv.

2. *What might you as coach do so that David is enabled to get the most value from this first session?*

## *The coaching*

David turns out to be in his late thirties, tall and balding. He has a quiet manner, polite but slightly cautious or reserved. He meets you in reception at exactly the time agreed, shakes hands and leads you down a short corridor to one of the pre-booked meeting rooms: plenty of windows and, unusually, well ventilated despite the hot weather. He indicates a seat for you at a glass conference table and sits two places further round to your left. Hot and cold drinks and a plate of biscuits nestle in the centre of the table, as does a large multi-function telephone. He takes his BlackBerry and places it carefully alongside his notepad.

Coach: Now, David, what would you like to achieve from this session?

David: Well, when I got your call, it rather caught me on the hop. I thought everything was going well so when I put the phone down I felt really confused. I guess I'd like to understand why I need coaching, what I need to do better and why. I know I've been off ill for some time but I've come back raring to go and I feel I've done a really good job. I've picked up all my previous clients; I've made contact with them all and my work's on target.

Coach: OK – well, the first thing to say is that having coaching isn't a criticism or a punishment. In fact around 75 per cent of the leaders of the top FTSE 100 companies have their own coach. (David raises a sceptical eyebrow.) It's about a neutral outsider helping you think about things that are of interest or concern and gain new insights. So one of the things I can help you do is use your past experience as you move into leadership.

Having spent some time helping David clear up his misconceptions about coaching and making sure he understands the process, you return to 'goals'.

Coach: So, looking again at goals, what would you like to be different as a result of this session?

David: I'd like to feel that people here appreciate my efforts. I've tried really hard to fit back in, to avoid anyone feeling they've got to carry me or protect me. They need to understand that I'm competent and not keep patronising me. I hate that. I've got a career to build. (He shifts slightly in his chair, glancing almost involuntarily at his BlackBerry.)

Coach: What sort of things have people actually said to you?

David: Well, just yesterday I rang Dawn – she's my internal company client and I've been doing some work for her about marketing a new product. She seemed really surprised to hear from me, even when I reminded her that I'm back in harness. It was almost as if I'd left or died or something. And when I asked her what was wrong, all she could do was tell me about how good the help she'd had from Sarah had been while I was off. And Sarah came up to me three times yesterday to say how good it was to have me back and what a good job I'm doing. Patronising or what! She'd never have done that before. I just gave her a dirty look and kept my mouth shut. But if it carries on, I'll definitely say something – even if it *is* to bite her head off!'

(There's a pause, several seconds of silence and David crosses his arms defiantly.)

Coach: What would you have liked Dawn and Sarah to say to you?

David: I'd have liked Dawn to deal with me in the business way we had before.

Coach: And how was that?

David: Well, usually she trusted me to get on with what she wanted . . .

Coach: You said, 'Usually'?

David: Well, there were a couple of times just before I went off sick that she reckoned my work wasn't 'up to scratch' as she charmingly put it. In fact she told Sarah about it and Sarah gave me a right old rollicking. Reckoned I was getting sloppy and missing deadlines. So I told her straight: 'No one's ever complained about my work or my efforts before. And I'm blowed if I'm going to take that from someone who's only just joined the company and doesn't know the first thing about my work.' Actually, with hindsight, maybe that wasn't the best thing to say in the circumstances. (He smiles slightly, his face relaxing almost imperceptibly. The overall effect though is remarkable, making him seem much more approachable, almost warm.)

Coach: So if Sarah came back in now and said that, with hindsight how would you like to have responded?
(There is a second period of silence.)
David: I don't know. I could tell from Sarah's reaction that she was angry. But then Dawn shouldn't have told tales to her, should she? (Again, his arms are folded and he moves back slightly into his chair. David's body language suggests he's tense.)
Coach: Why do you think Dawn did talk to Sarah?
David: Well, she was angry and thought she'd get her own back.
Coach: What other reasons do you think she might have had?
David: . . . Um, maybe she thought I needed a good wake-up call.
Coach: How do you feel about that?
David: It offends me.
Coach: It offends you?
David: Yes. It implies I'm not doing the best I can, I'm slacking, not up to the job.
Coach: So if Sarah had said that to you directly, how would you have replied?
(There's a long pause as David reflects.)
David: OK. Perhaps that wasn't the best piece of work I've ever given her. (He shifts slightly in his chair.)
Coach: 'Perhaps that wasn't the best piece of work . . .?'
David: To be honest, I remember I was feeling under a bit of pressure at the time. And I hadn't been sleeping so well, so I was really tired. (You notice a couple of beads of sweat form on his forehead.) Maybe it did affect the quality a little bit.
Coach: So if you were to have that conversation again with Sarah, how would you now want it to go? What would you want to say?

David: I guess I'd want to tackle it even earlier. I'd want to let Dawn know that perhaps she had a point . . . But it won't happen again because now I'm back I'm on top of the game again! (He looks silently out of the window, perhaps sensing there had been just a little too much emphasis in his last words to be completely convincing. But you let him take the time to think. There's another period of silence.)

Coach: So if I summarise what I think you've just said so far: you were under some pressure at the time and so perhaps the piece of work wasn't as good as it might have been. But you resent the fact that Dawn reported that to Sarah rather than you. And you think your response to Sarah wasn't what it might have been. But now you're back on top of your game again . . . (David nods, a little uncertainly. There's a pause as he reflects.)

Coach: Earlier on, you said Sarah's attitude was different since you've come back. Why do you think that's altered?

David: Well, I guess she thinks that I might not be able to do the job, to 'stand the pressure'. (He indicates the quotation-marks with his fingers in the air). She reckons she won't get the standard of work she wants. But I'll make damn sure she does!

Coach: What else might have made her attitude different?

David: What do you mean?

Coach: Can you think of any other reasons why she might seem to be different?

David: I don't follow.

Coach: Well, might I offer a suggestion? Maybe she doesn't want to over-burden you and put you under the old pressure again. Do you think that's possible?

David: I guess so. But I'm not doing this for her. Or even for me. It's for my kids and I guess for my wife as well. I want them to have all the things in life I didn't. They're still quite young and we want to give them the best schools and to support lots of interests. Those all cost money.

34 SETTING THE SCENE

Coach: You're doing this for your family? So what exactly do you want to give them?
David: It *is* about giving them the best. That's it in a nutshell.

For the remainder of this session, you explore with David how he thinks his wife and then his children would define 'best' as he slowly begins to recognise that there might be a difference between his definition and theirs. You charge him with finding out before the next session.

> **Activity**
> - Underline all the words that might be about 'meaning' in this section of dialogue. What do you notice? If you were able to re-run it, make a list of the questions you would ask at those points. How might the outcome be different?
> - Towards the end of the dialogue, David's coach asks him how his family might define 'best'. Why do you think the coach asked that question at this point?

It is now half-way through the fourth session. The following points have emerged:

- David is beginning to recognise that he had been struggling for some time, even before he went off sick, 'feeling for the first time in my life that I was on the brink of failing'; he'd been highly successful in OMG.
- At one point, looking back, he summarised it as 'been there, done that, got the proverbial tee-shirt'. When you challenged him on that, he admitted that he'd perhaps been a little complacent in his work, which led him to make some mistakes.
- He's also begun to recognise that he resents Sarah because she was appointed over him. After probing, he realises that actually he probably didn't actually want the job, more that as the 'rising star' he wasn't given the chance. You've explored that with him and he's realised a growing sense of losing focus in his career, of feeling there's no challenge but not really knowing what he wants to do next. After a

few questions around this, it's clear that he's not particularly keen on getting more responsibility in OMG or indeed in a similar company but that he feels something is currently missing, that he's lost his previous drive.

## *The coaching*

Coach: David – a couple of minutes ago, you said something about not feeling that you belong in OMG any more. What exactly did you mean?

David: Well, I think it's less to do with anything in OMG changing as me. I still feel it's the right place to be, but something in me feels different and I need to understand what that is, what it means.

Coach: OK – so can you think of an image or symbol that might show what you're feeling?

David: Funny you should say that! Last week I took the kids to a fair at the local showground. They really wanted a go on the shooting range but they're far too young so I said I'd do it and they could tell me what to do! Anyway, I was lining up the sights on those wretched ducks that keep popping up on jets of water and then dropping back down just when you think you've got them all lined up to fire. Struck me that's just how my life feels at the moment. It made me laugh so much I completely missed – the kids thought it was great! But actually, the idea of getting all my ducks in a row in my life kind of appeals.

Coach: So . . .?

David: I know – 'What would that look like?' I can hear you asking it! Trouble is, I've no idea. There seem to be too many choices, too many things I could do. But I don't want to end up in a blind alley with no answers. How do I make sense of it?

Coach: Well, there's an image that some people have found helpful. Shall I explain it and you can see if it makes any sense of what you're feeling?

David: Sure.

Coach: It's called The Existential Leap. Don't pull a face – it's not as bad as it sounds! The suggestion is that we have two distinct and fundamentally different phases or drivers in our life. The first one, the Warrior, is where we feel driven to succeed, to establish who we are and to shape out our unique space and place, what we bring that's different to what other people bring. It's about achieving at work, finding a 'mate' and succeeding; it's about separation and delineation. The second phase of life is called the Elder, where we perhaps feel more of a drive to put things back rather than take things out; we know much about who we are as an individual, know we feel a drive to understand who we are in relation to other people, our links and connectivity with them rather than what separates us out from them. The longer we explore in this second phase, the more we see and understand connectivity with each other and can feel integrated into it.[22]

David: Hmmm. Yes, that's interesting. I can definitely see a link. So you're suggesting I'm at that crossroads, the end of the first phase?'

Coach: Well, it's not called a crossroads, it's a bit more stark and challenging than that. It's described as The Existential Leap, the idea of jumping off a precipice, the place that we've become familiar with, into the unknown!

David: (He laughs.) Oh great! So it's a leap out into the unknown with the enticement of being dashed on the rocks if you fail to reach the other side!'

Coach: Perhaps! But it's also an invitation to leave behind some of the old dissatisfactions and begin to find some other meanings. The trouble is, a lot of people don't have the courage to challenge their current assumptions and beliefs. The edge is marked by the Existential Question: 'What sort of person do you want to be when you're grown up?'! Answers next time we meet, please: you did say you were up for a challenge!

David: Yes – but not that big! No, seriously, it does sound interesting.

Coach: So what can I do now that would be most helpful at this point?

David: I think I want to explore that phrase 'belonging' a bit more. Why do I suddenly feel I'm not being true to myself? I never used to feel like that and as far as I can see, nothing's really changed. Yet you're telling me I'm on the precipice, the edge of a huge leap. And I think that *feels* right. It just doesn't make sense . . .

---

### Activity

- At which points is David himself now beginning to raise questions of 'meaning'? Where might the coach have followed this up? Take one of these opportunities and describe how it might have evolved if it had followed the 'meaning' route.
- Once the coach did explore these, how did this benefit David? What else might the coach ask to make it even more effective?
- In the light of the issues raised here, if you were to continue coaching David around the search for meaning, what questions would you ask and why?
- Each time you see the word 'silence' in the dialogue review what has just happened and consider what alternative approaches the coach might have employed next and how this might have affected the remaining stages of the coaching process.

---

We'll return to this case study in later chapters.

## Part 3: Spirituality

David's vague feelings of dissatisfaction are echoed by many in the workplace and beyond. They represent a sense of something deeper even than a search for meaning; something other than the imminent. Typically this is a growing awareness of the needs and aspirations of those beyond our own narrow self-interests and those of our family, the sense of belonging to something greater. Alongside this growing awareness is the growing desire to do something about it, to put something back, to make a difference and to leave a legacy. This is the search for the *transcendent* meaning of work, the things that Herzberg terms satisfaction-building, and that are closer to what I term the *spiritual* search.

> **Box 2.5**
>
> Some years ago I was part of a team of 20 working on a bid for a multi-million-pound contract to outsource services from a Local Authority, a genuine opportunity to make a difference to people's lives in the delivery of frontline services. The deadline loomed ever larger but the work pile never seemed to diminish. Pressure rose. Internal deadlines were missed. Working days lengthened into nights and early mornings. Those around us in the office could feel the tension mounting until finally the deadline was reached like the finishing tape of a marathon. A sense of anti-climax and exhaustion cut in. Until, that is, we heard we'd won it!
>
> In the debrief some ten days later, one of the team was asked to describe what it felt like at that moment. 'The best feeling ever! Knowing I'd been a part of that successful team, having their support and encouragement, even in – especially in – the difficult times. It was almost spiritual: it just brought us so much closer as a team and brought the best out of us. Fantastic! Can't wait for the next one!'

The team member in Box 2.5 isn't unique in describing intense team-building and team-operating as a spiritual experience. But what exactly do they mean? That's the theme of this section and the heart of the book.

If *meaning* relates to Maslow's levels 3 and 4,[23] then see the definition of *spirituality* in Box 2.6.

> **Box 2.6**
>
> *Spirituality* is that part of the search to do with recognition of something outside and greater than ourselves.

The 'greater good' relates to Maslow's level 5 (Self-actualisation). It is essentially an activity of the heart or the spirit.

It is *spirituality* that defines us as a species, drives the desire to make a positive difference to others and sets us apart from other species in seeking answers to the metaphysical question of 'why?' and answers it in the context of 'our need to place our enterprises in a frame of wider meaning and purpose'.[24]

Spirituality is also that which pertains to the relationship between the divine and the human. It is about the relationship itself rather than the outward manifestations of that relationship. To confuse the two can lead to unhelpful distractions. The warm glow of belonging to that work team in the story in Box 2.5 tells us much about the importance of forging interconnected relationships, but it is an outward manifestation, not a spiritual experience. The *feelings* may be similar to those of a divine-human relationship but the *source* is not the same. That team spirit and its outward manifestations could just as plausibly have been rooted in greed, drive for success, aggression, fear of losing one's job.

Suppose we push this story further and consider it from the perspective of the business organisation. The organisation might conclude that the transcending business value to both the team and to the clients was that the work would make a real difference to improving the quality of people's lives. It might then decide to make this a more prominent feature of its future business. It might take the working relationship values identified so positively in the debrief and roll them out across the company, placing a higher profile on the intrinsic value of what it was doing and why: seeking to bring out the best in colleagues and transformation in clients.

This would certainly fall in the realm of my earlier definition of *meaning*: 'the making sense of situations, from which we derive our psychological or moral sense, purpose, or significance'. But it does not qualify as spiritual. What might have transformed it into the spiritual? The presence of words such as 'vocation'; 'mission'; 'transformation' (of self or others); 'legacy'; 'greater power'; 'greater purpose'; 'something external drawing us'; 'the greater good'? Perhaps. This gets a little closer to recognising what *spirituality* entails and it would certainly identify some of the *functions* of spirituality, to:

- define our humanity;
- help us discover a wider meaning and purpose;
- question why we are doing what we are doing;
- challenge us to want our lives to make a difference.

In essence – it moves us into a new dimension.

## *From the horizontal to the vertical*

The desire to make a difference to those around us is certainly a component of spirituality. But it is not the defining characteristic. There are two different axes in play. If the search for meaning constitutes a horizontal axis, there is a vertical axis: the search for spirituality. The end of the axes represents the focus of outlook. The horizontal focuses on the interconnectivity of my place in humanity and the obligations thus

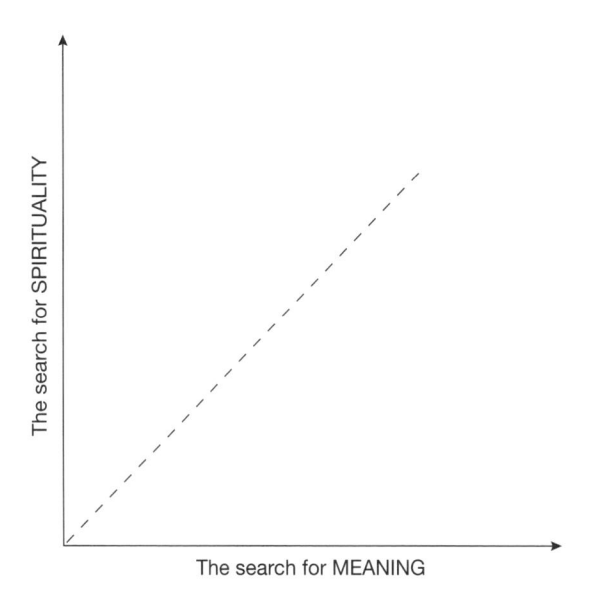

*Figure 2.3* **The search for meaning and spirituality**

placed upon me. The vertical focuses me on a Higher Power, above and beyond (transcending) humanity, calling or drawing me to do what I do as part of my relating to that Higher Power.

Thus the quest is, at one level, seeking the equilibrium, the convergence of the two. But it's more complicated than that, and we'll return to further refinements as the book progresses.

Crucially, spirituality is about awareness of and response to something external and more significant. Jay Conger agues that 'spirituality *lifts us beyond ourselves and our narrow self-interests* ... It helps us to see our deeper connections to one another and to the world beyond ourselves'.[25] Research suggests that spirituality is an innate need to connect to something larger than ourselves, something we instinctively recognise as divine or sacred and yearn to possess.[26]

How we search for this and describe that quest and its progress may vary considerably: connection with Nature or the Universe, through art, medicine, music, through seeking a noble path or beauty.

Many psychologists have argued that spirituality is actually a necessary part of full human development. Ursula King, for example, writes: 'Spirituality is now understood anthropologically as an exploration into what is involved in becoming fully human.'[27] We ignore it at our peril. Recent research suggests that there are stages of spiritual development much akin to those in physical and psychological development (see Chapters 3 and 7). Part of the role of coaching can be to facilitate movement from one stage to another.

So this is getting closer to what sets spirituality apart from meaning. The search for *meaning* is an inquisitive quest for understanding and purpose. The search for *spirituality* is an acquisitive quest responding to a yearning recognition of the existence of something/someone greater that seeks active participation and engagement, which attracts in order to empower. It is an activity of the heart or the spirit. Spirituality is 'the way in which people connect the activities of their daily life with their wellsprings of deepest meaning.'[28]

## *Summary so far*

*Meaning* operates *horizontally*: it is what we draw from our experiences across humanity, the way in which we organise them and explain them in order to make sense of them – at least to our own satisfaction. *Spirituality* operates *vertically*, linking us into meaning but taking us beyond it into terminology typically expressing recognition of something larger than and beyond oneself.

> **Box 2.7**
>
> For the next section of this book, I'm going to build on these points:
>
> - *meaning* as a *horizontal* activity, our inquisitive quest for understanding across humanity to see connections and purpose
> - *spirituality* as a *vertical* activity, our innate need to connect to something larger than and external to ourselves – something divine or sacred

> **Activity**
>
> The core concepts of spirituality include meaning, wholeness, integrity, interconnectedness, creativity, a sense of 'greater' and transformation. In the light of this, what might you identify as 'spiritual' in your life at the moment?

## *Spiritual Intelligence (SQ)*

Emerging research into Emotional Intelligence (EQ) has been one of the most important developments of the past few decades in business, raising awareness of the significance of feelings and emotions and their impact. It has shone a flashlight internally, causing much to be illuminated. But it has shone the spotlight internally; it has not shone the beam of illumination too far externally.

MEANING AND SPIRITUA...

The emerging concept of Spiritual Intelligence
it to a new dimension that has major implications fc
effectiveness.[29] If EQ allows me to assess the situa...
which I operate and respond, SQ raises questions about
whether I should be there in the first place and prompts me
to ask this in a context of connectedness to those around me
and to a Higher Power. Cindy Wigglesworth defines SQ as 'the
ability to behave with Compassion and Wisdom while maintaining inner and outer peace (equanimity) regardless of the
circumstances';[30] it is about both doing and being especially
under pressure and is one of the reasons why spiritually
intelligent leaders are so respected.

Zohar and Marshall make a further distinction: 'unlike
IQ, which orients itself with respect to rules, and EQ, which
is guided by the situation in which it finds itself, SQ lights our
way to what mystics have called "the eye of the heart"'.[31]
Spirituality is about connecting with our spirit, our source of
being and then recognising how that impacts motivation,
aspiration and application in every element of life, clearly
relevant for our role as coaches.

> **Activity**
>
> What questions can you formulate that might help a coachee begin to recognise and explore these issues?

## *Corridors and rooms*

While these are important areas in their own right, my contention is that they are means to an end, corridors leading to a room rather than the room itself. In this context, a corridor refers to a place of transition; a room refers to a destination. There are numerous corridors down which the coachee may be approaching issues around meaning and spirituality: *ethics* (a feeling of dissatisfaction with current behaviour of self, organisation or others; a recognition of interconnectedness perhaps via stewardship of world resources as manifested in concern for climate change or fair trade issues); *reorientation* (success is not satisfying what I thought it would satisfy); *disorientation* (an external traumatic event that prompts reflection, such as a bereavement; birth of a child; missed promotion); *transition* (developmentally reaching the boundaries of the next life stage either chronologically or emotionally). These are dealt with in subsequent chapters.

It can be difficult to open the door to a room designated 'spiritual'; it can be difficult even to spot points of entry, as if the doors have been wallpapered over when a fashion changed! Previously the corridor might have been via the religious imperatives of dominant Christianity or the great Institutions. 'Religion' used to provide the corridor to a sense of purpose, belonging and contributing but it is no longer dominant in people's lives in the same way and no longer has the same imperative. These corridors have become roads less travelled. But rejection of the outward expression (religion) has not taken away the deeper need to search for that 'room' labelled meaning, belonging, contributing and the Higher Power. But now the corridors can seem lonely, shadowy and threatening. Small wonder many avoid them. A reflective coaching companion on that journey can be a valuable asset and amongst other benefits can help maintain both internal and external perspective.

The sense of belonging to and contributing to something greater than oneself, doing things for others rather than for oneself, commonly results in a greater sense of well-being. Without that reflection, we are likely to fall short of our potential and to feel its loss.

### Box 2.8

Once upon a time, a small remote village was visited by a travelling circus. All the villagers marvelled at the freedom of the performers as they flew through the air, the skills of the jugglers as they hurled and caught skittles, swords and even small children from the audience. They laughed with the clowns and cheered the horse riders. The circus folk thrilled them with their joy, their exuberance, their freedom and their skills. Then they were gone.

But a day or so later a small baby was found abandoned just outside the village. No one could explain how it had survived. But survive it had. And despite exhaustive enquiries, no one could find where the circus people had moved on to. It was almost as if they'd never existed. Only the memories of the villagers and the presence of the baby said otherwise. And so the child was taken in and cared for by a childless farmer and his wife.

The baby grew, became a toddler and then a child. And the more she grew, the more the villagers began to notice her differences. Her hair was deep black and shiny, quite unlike the blond hair of the others. Her nose was long and pointed, quite unlike the short, flat noses of her companions. And she was tall, thin and athletic, easily out-running and out-wrestling even most of the boys who were much shorter and plumper. Her duties of cooking and cleaning and mending increased. She was popular, well fed and contented.

Until, of course, the circus returned. If anyone noticed the physical similarities between the girl and the slim circus athletes, no one said anything. Even the girl herself seemed unaware. But as she gazed and marvelled at their prowess, she turned to the farmer beside her. 'How graceful they are, how free and how skilled.'

'Ah yes,' sighed the farmer. 'They are beholden to no one. Their time and their life are their own. They are free to come and go, travel, to practice and to perform as they please. And all welcome them. They are people of freedom and the theatre. You have to be born to that. We are people of the land.'

And so the girl lived and died in that village, one of the people of the land. *Because that's what she thought she was.*

Self-limiting beliefs so often force us to look down or to look in. The-sky's-the-limit thinking, conversely, frees us up; ridiculously over-inflated beliefs can often lead people to achieve the seemingly impossible. The quest for spirituality challenges us to look up, to reframe the false boundaries we've been told or have believed that limit our potential – especially when we long to fly and soar!

## Summary

In these sections, I have argued that the search for spirituality is a step further than the search for meaning; indeed Maslow later added it as a further dimension to his hierarchy of needs.[32] I have also argued that meaning operates on one axis (horizontal) while spirituality operates on two (horizontal and vertical). This is the added value of spirituality. It offers the enticing prospect of empowerment, connection and passion to make a difference. There is already a plethora of material dealing with the search for meaning; also, many of the points about spirituality will apply to meaning but not vice versa. Finally, I've suggested that there is a continuum of development through the multiple intelligences and within SQ itself and that our coachees may be starting at any point on the continuum. The remainder of the book will refer predominantly to spirituality rather than to meaning.

To return to our circus story in Box 2.8, let's now see how the orphan might have fared had she been blessed with a coach in some activities.

## Part 4: Further activities

- Are there any mottos that guide you in your personal life?
- List the organisations and people with whom you spend most of your time, both in work (paid or voluntarily) and beyond. What issue/s would drive you out onto the street in protest – and why? What priorities might you establish/have you established for spending your money? If you had a fortune, what differences would that make? What values and priorities do these reveal?
- If you could pick an animal that symbolises your current spending patterns, what would it be? (Where we spend our money gives some indication of our current situation and priorities and hence our values.)
- Consider what terminology (in the case studies and in your responses) might indicate a 'gateway opportunity' as discussed in Chapter 1. The following list might help.

Accountability
Achievement
Advancement
Adventure
Affection
Allegiance
Authenticity
Belonging
Challenge
Collaboration
Commitment
Community
Competitiveness
Contribution
Co-operation
Creativity
Diversity
Duty
Economic security
Ego-self
Empowerment
Ethical business
Excitement
Faith
Fame
Family Happiness
Freedom
Flexibility
Friendship
Generosity
Health
Helpfulness
Higher Power
Higher Self
Honesty
Honour
Independence
Inner Harmony
Innovation
Inspirational
Integration
Integrity
Intuition
Involvement
Learning
Loyalty
Making a difference
Mission
Openness
Passion
Peace
Personal development
Physical challenge
Pleasure
Power
Purpose
Quality
Recognition
Respect for others
Respect for self
Responsibility
Risk
Security
Self-actualisation
Sharing
Soul
Spirituality
Status
Success
Support
Transformation
Trust
Variety
Wealth
Wholeness
Wisdom
Yearning

## *Gateway phrases you might hear*

- Does it really matter, in the broader scale of things?
- Is there more than just the here-and-now?
- What am I called to do?
- Who am I called to be?
- I want them to have faith in me.

# Part Two

## Putting into practice

# 3

# Spirituality and work-life balance

## Overview

Chapter 2 drew the distinction between *meaning* (as 'a horizontal activity, an inquisitive quest for understanding, connection and purpose') and *spirituality* ('an innate need to connect to something larger than ourselves, something divine or sacred'), with the latter equating to Maslow's Level 5 Self-actualisation and providing the vertical axis to meaning's horizontal. This chapter applies these ideas in practical coaching environments and starts with something many people claim to be struggling with: developing and maintaining a healthy work-life balance. The chapter contains four parts. Part 1 asks what work-life balance actually means and suggests it be rephrased as *The Balanced Life*; it examines the impact of life-stages and the impact of time and of stress. Part 2 deals with the search for meaning and the importance of happiness, well-being, satisfaction and the exercise of signature strengths. Part 3 develops this into spirituality and how this expresses itself with 'right roads' and 'dark woods', as well as the impact of developing Spiritual Intelligence and energy as part of The Balanced Life. It shifts the focus beyond narrow self-interest through interconnectivity vertically into the sacred, the divine, and the implications for how life is lived. Finally, Part 4 contains several practical activities to help the reader broaden their own understanding of these concepts and provides some tools to deploy them.

## Part 1: Work–life balance

The last five decades or so have presented more *choices* in everyday life than probably any other era in human history. Yet there has been less *guidance* on how to select from a confusing plethora of options. The ensuing uncertainty about whether these are the 'right' choices and whether they will result in satisfaction, well-being or happiness often creates a sense that things are neither right nor the way we would wish them to be. Little wonder that workdays lost through stress are rising rapidly,[1] alongside a growing sense that things are out of balance.

Those who feel a lack of this balance rarely argue that anything is missing and needs adding: it's not a case of looking for more energy or more physical strength or even more hours in the day. It is almost always about realigning existing priorities with deepest values and beliefs; it is a qualitative issue. There is recognition that 'life' is not just the remnant left over once 'work' has gobbled its fill. There are other components apart from work: family, friends, relaxation, leisure, entertainment, etc. And there is recognition that without appropriate attention each of these areas diminishes energy and reduces effectiveness. There is also a recognition that we contribute to the lives of others, that their lives are also incomplete without our presence as is ours in their absence. We not only take, we also contribute.

At the same time, there seems to be a widespread sense of uncertainty. Frankl[2] noted: 'It is a peculiarity of man that he can only live by looking to the future'. It is one of our greatest assets, allowing us to plan, prepare, and identify options. But it is also one of our greatest curses, encouraging the illusion that we therefore can somehow have unlimited power to manipulate that future to serve our individualistic desires. The future to which we look is increasingly complex and unclear and those institutions that previously might have provided the signposts (Church, State, Parliament) are increasingly undermined, discredited or dismissed. We understand that all is not as we might wish. We understand there is a lack of balance.

Understanding what we feel is one thing. Doing something about it is quite another. This requires change. And many find change uncomfortable. It requires energy and commitment. A significant number of people are unable or unwilling to challenge or go beyond the assumptions and foundations upon which their worldview is founded (what South American tribes call their 'mythic entrancement':[3] being constrained by the limitations of their own cultural assumptions and views). The role of the coach in this context is to help the coachee challenge their assumptions and explore their noble goals,[4] their deeper aspirations and longings so that they are enriched for their choices rather than constrained within their mythic entrancement. Noble goals reveal much about values and beliefs, sense of purpose and meaning, the alignment and satisfaction of which will be a crucial element in helping people feel their lives have balance.

## *What is The Balanced Life?*

US business-writer Stephen Covey summed up the fundamental aspirations of a balanced and fulfilling life as to 'live, love, learn and leave a legacy'.[5] Sounds pretty straightforward: life is just a matter of balancing. And it's clearly of interest to many people: an internet search for 'work-life balance' identifies in excess of 51 million links. Yet a recent Gallup survey of 27,000 EU adults revealed that 51 per cent claimed to find it difficult to combine work and family life.[6] For a significant number of people it seems as if it's less about balance than about juggling.

The UK's National Institute for Clinical Excellence recently published guidelines *Promoting Well-Being in the Workplace* and concluded that mental ill health costs the country some £38bn a year. They also concluded that staff presenteeism (physically present but mentally and emotionally absent) accounted for one and a half times the cost of absenteeism, some £18bn. It was most prevalent amongst senior management.

This suggests that not only do many people feel a mismatch between their aspiration to 'live, love, learn and leave a legacy' and the reality in which they find themselves but also that the resulting sense of imbalance is not simply an internal confusion but also negatively impacts external performance. The impact and financial cost for the workplace in terms of absenteeism, sickness and diminishing motivation and its impact on productivity and loyalty is immense. Its cost outside the workplace in terms of strain on relationships and ultimate life expectancy can only be imagined. Little wonder that organisations are giving it an increasing profile.[7] The benefits are mutual: a 2009 survey by talent management firm Morgan Redwood[8] concluded that business earnings could be increased by 23 per cent if staff enjoy a healthy work-life balance.

This section focuses on our deep struggle to find sense and fulfilment in what we do and why we do it. It challenges our obligations and responsibilities. It takes us into what we want and need from life for ourselves and for others in order to feel satisfied. It challenges us over how we spend that most valuable of our commodities, time, and asks whether we are currently getting 'value for money'. As such, it is a vitally important area for coaches to pursue with clients.

At the same time it potentially blurs and spans the oft-separated realms of executive (business) coaching and life coaching. By 'life coaching' in this context I mean dealing holistically, the whole person rather than just that part manifested in the workplace. I make no apologies for that, since it seems to me that the separation is largely a matter of convenience rather than substance anyway. That rather synthetic distinction is also true of the next few chapters in this book: they exist separately primarily to break down some of the material into more manageable chunks and are simply some of the 'corridors' that I referred to in Chapter 2 that might lead into the 'room' of spirituality.

Let me also say from the outset that I find the phrase 'work-life balance' deeply unhelpful. It implies that 'work' and 'life' are different and mutually-excluding; it implies that life only begins and exists outside work; it assumes that what happens inside work is a sort of suspended animation, a zombie-like existence. And, yes, I know some people feel *exactly* like that about their jobs! But I want to challenge the underlying assumption that there's a dichotomy. And then I want to suggest (and develop in Chapter 6) that it's as important to search for meaning and spirituality while at work as it is at play. Hence, I shall use the more-positive term: *The Balanced Life*.

The phrase suggests there's a juggling act or a seesaw: there are conflicting demands, expectations, needs and benefits and that these are in constant flux, requiring a constant vigilance and a continual readjustment. It necessitates our deliberate intervention, struggle even, to avoid finding ourselves suddenly catapulted into the air to land in pain and confusion with an almighty unpleasant crash! That much at least seems true. And many are the weights keen to descend from a great height on to the opposite side of our seesaw.

But a seesaw also requires a pivotal point against which these things are weighed and balanced. That's where meaning comes in. Those who have found a profound sense of meaning for themselves do seem able to maintain balance longer and to greater effect.

One final point: while balance *is* important, it's not the whole story. Complete balance can mean inertia and as the seesaw metaphor shows, after a while inertia may not be much fun either . . .

## *Life stages, personality and generations*

What constitutes an appropriately Balanced Life is likely to be different for individuals at different life stages. It is also likely to be defined differently by different personality types. Even different generations can have radically different perceptions of what constitutes a Balanced Life for them.

Sometimes there might be a need to proactively emphasise one component by our own intervention: sometimes we need to challenge equilibrium in order to pursue the search for meaning and spirit in the different dimensions of life. Sometimes the balance may be disturbed by factors beyond our control.

Many currently popular tools for exploring personality and its implications stress the importance of answering their questions in terms of both work and leisure contexts[9] in order to discern the fullest picture. They recognise the importance of identifying our core needs, motives and abilities in each dimension and where or even whether these are currently being met. The plan is to proactively ensure that those not met in one dimension are met in another; or are planned for later; or are consciously postponed – to ensure that the parts literally do add up to the whole. For clarity they are often grouped under headings concerning the development of Body, Mind, Heart and Soul (or Spirit). These roughly equate with Covey's quartet of 'Live, Learn, Love and Legacy'.[10]

These quadrants can be used to further develop the model of the two axes of spirituality and meaning from Chapter 2 (see Figure 3.1).

The quadrants don't develop strictly sequentially; it isn't necessary to complete the full development of Body in order to begin development of Mind, for example. They are

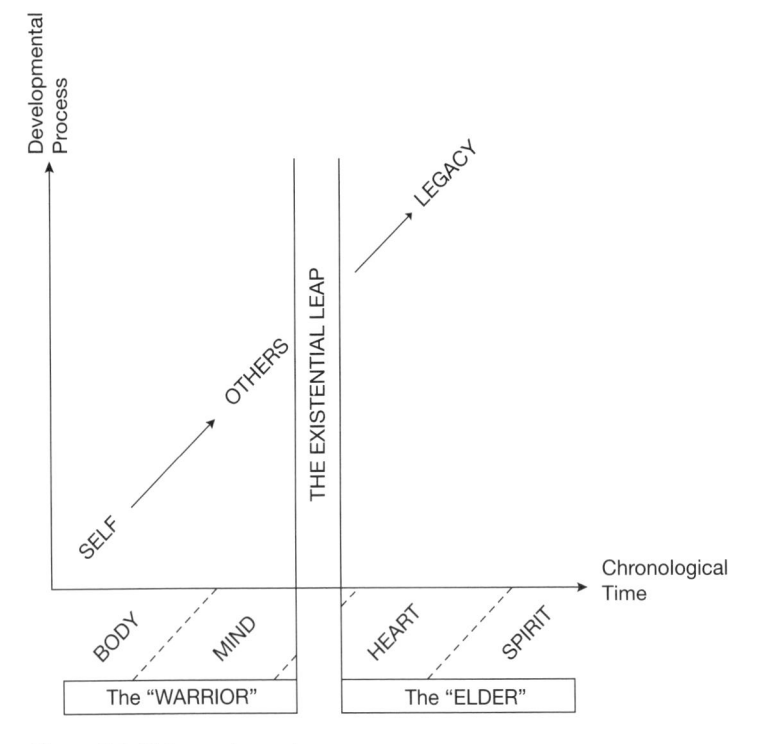

*Figure 3.1* **Elder and warrior**

not sequential but they are interrelated and developmental. We're unlikely to undertake much significant development of Mind (in an intellectual sense) until we have mastered at least *some* of the basics of Body. At the same time, developing these takes place within a broader progression spanning out from the inherent Self-centeredness of our early life through an awareness of Others that is initially manipulative (how can I get them to provide what I need from them) and then gradually interactive (I both take and give). The quadrants also relate to The Existential Leap. It would be tempting to consider The Existential Leap as the defining progression into the Quadrants of Heart and Spirit and there is some truth in that since a safe landing on the other side does indeed shift the focus from Body and Mind self-centeredness into these two essentially other-focused quadrants. But interestingly in my experience those who make the leap commonly also experience a renewed interest in developing Body and Mind: it is the motivation and purpose that has changed and become focused on doing so in order to better help others.

It's possible to seek 'balance' whatever the quadrant but how that is expressed and lived out is likely to be very different. *The Balanced Life* might also be defined differently between different personality types (e.g. between those who 'work to live' or 'live to work'). It might also be different between different generations: the expectations of baby-boomers are often significantly different from those of Generation X/Y (see below). For example, while many baby-boomers rate being able to choose to continue working beyond the normal retirement age as a high priority, Generation X seek different priorities: A MORI Poll (July 2003) asked 1,000 final year students at 25 UK universities about their career priorities. Rated at number 3 was salary and training; at number 2, working in the public sector rather than blue-chip (an interesting insight into 'values'); and at number 1, work-life balance! In the midst of the ongoing financial crisis, it's unclear whether new entrants to the job market will be more willing to accept a less positive balance in order to simply obtain employment. But the evidence suggests that as soon as conditions ease those employers who took unfair advantage will soon lose that talent to rival companies. There is growing recognition that while we may intentionally choose delayed gratification, the resulting energy-draining position can only be maintained for a limited period without suffering lasting damage.

At the risk of stating the obvious, it's also worth pointing out that 'work' is not necessarily the same as 'employment'. The sweating athlete in training, the physical demands of redecorating a room, the emotional commitment of volunteering in a home for the elderly are all clearly 'work' and all can be carried on to excess so that they over-balance the seesaw. But for convenience I shall follow the conventional usage in referring to work as meaning paid employment.

What constitutes balance may also differ over time: for the young family of three growing children and jobs it will be different to 30 years later when the children live elsewhere and jobs may be a thing of the past. And how that family defines a balanced life may be very different from their neighbours, who to all intents and purposes face exactly the same challenges. A worker might agree to spend a limited time working abroad away from family in order to secure more advantageous conditions upon return, sacrificing the short-term preference of more time with family or friends. Providing it is agreed and bounded it potentially has little negative impact on the feeling that life is balanced.

One final point. A big part of the fun of the seesaw is the jolt that comes from sudden alterations in the balance: being shaken out of the comfort-zone of complacent equilibrium may be no bad thing for some coachees.

But more generally, why is this seesaw a balancing act so tricky that at least half of us feel we're getting it wrong, wishing it were different, yet feel unable to redress the balance?

## *Time*

Is this fundamentally an issue of time-management? Certainly there are myriad books seeking to convince us so. It fits our preference for neat explanations and readily applicable solutions. It seems to make sense. And it appeals to our need to feel there's a better future. If we could just work harder or longer now there's better balance with shorter working hours, less pressure, more security and perhaps more pay – just around the corner. There are two common paradoxes revealed here: first, very often that corner never seems to be reached and remains hovering just beyond reach; second, working longer hours doesn't necessarily increase the productivity being sought. And choosing to work longer hours rarely improves satisfaction. Interestingly, according to a recent Stanford University study,[11] neither does multi-tasking, doing more things at the same time: they discovered that far from wringing more productivity from each hour, habitual multitaskers actually perform less well because of the extra mental and emotional resources needed to retain one set of information and process that alongside one or more others. Even creating more time for our preferred activities such as leisure doesn't necessarily work.

Effective time management is a means, not an end. It is a tool to carve more space in order to accommodate energy-generating activities. Returning to the earlier analogy of the four quadrants, 'better time management' can often be a solution of the Head to issues more readily applicable to the Heart and the Spirit. The issue may not be one of improved efficiency so much as re-channelled energy and re-examined priorities. Perhaps there is something deeper and more profound going on.

We commit the majority of our time to that which we believe to be our highest priorities. However, that which requires our greatest commitment at any given point may not be the same as that which we consider the most important or satisfying. The reason for something ranking number one priority may simply be the need to stay with an organisation (however toxic its culture) because of the need to earn in order to live. It is a high cost to pay: the workplace gets a much-reduced efficiency and commitment and the worker loses any sense of fulfilment.

One of the most valuable contributions a coach can make is to help clients explore the degree to which they do (or do not) have control over these issues. The Work Foundation calls this 'Time Sovereignty',[12] the opportunity to control our allocation of our time, work and workload, including where, when and how that work takes place.

## *Stress*

Over the past decade or so numerous government and other agencies have been regularly releasing research emphasising the importance of creating and maintaining mental, physical and emotional energy and warning of the life-shortening, energy-draining effects of stress. (They have yet to include spiritual.)

For example, a CIPD/HSE[13] Survey in 2006 reported that about half a million people in the UK experience work-related stress. Of course, not all of this is a *Balanced Life* issue; a bomb-disposal expert might well report feeling work-related stress even if they have very generous leave-periods. A call-centre operative with silent telephones and no other work to do may suffer the stresses of boredom and an uncertain future.

Point 5: *The Balanced Life is a personal, pragmatic and negotiated response to the interconnected influences of personal circumstances, life-stage, job role and corporate environment in order to create at this point in time an acceptable sense of 'live, love, learn and leave a legacy'.*

In summary, choice in defining and flexibility in achieving an immediate Balanced Life enables focus on coping with short-term buffeting (economic imperative; child-birth readjustment; bereavement; even a lottery win) and in providing a more distant navigation point upon which to remain focused, however distant that may currently seem. Identifying what that distant navigation point might be returns us to the twin themes of this book: *meaning* and *spirituality*.

## Part 2: The search for meaning

In the 2008 CIPD/*Coaching at Work* annual Meaning and Purpose Survey,[14] one respondent noted: 'In a corporate environment . . . issues of confidence, self-esteem, motivation and happiness are emerging . . . Many of my clients are seeing their goals linking in with the bigger picture and their life and do not wish to separate these from work'. In essence, this is about meaning. In response to a recent Gallup Poll question:[15] '*How important to you is the belief that your life has meaning and purpose?*' 84 per cent said 'very important' and a further 15 per cent 'fairly important'. . .

What constitutes 'meaning' will vary from person to person and even from hour to hour, along with our expectations. Writing about his experiences as a survivor of World War II concentration camps, Viktor Frankl asserts that the quest to find a meaning was a prime factor in whether an individual survived the labour camps or not. In those camps it was pointless to dwell on what one had a right to expect in terms of a balanced life. In fact, he flips the question. 'It did not really matter what we expected from life, but rather what life expected from us.'[16] Surviving suffering is possible only by finding meaning. Indeed, he writes that, 'Man's search for meaning is the primary motivation in his life'.[17]

When all else is stripped away, that which is left is that which is most important to us. That is where we find our meaning; that is the first part of our quest. But if we then flip the question to ask, 'And what does that require of me?' we begin to exercise and develop our Spiritual Intelligence or SQ. In essence, this brings us to the difference between *meaning* (how we make sense of life) and *spirituality* (what life and its Higher Power expects *from* us).

In fact, The Balanced Life is about discovering where our deepest meaning lies and consequently what this then requires of us and then seeking this in each component that collectively makes up the totality of our life over a period of time. It's about integration rather than compartmentalisation.

The next chapter deals with this from the perspectives of crises – events that happen to us usually as a result of triggers beyond our control. Here, in the context of the work-life balance, it's from the perspective that we have a significant degree of control, even though we may not initially realise it or may choose not to exercise that control. The point is that the issues of The Balanced Life are often brought about by very *positive* drivers such as a new relationship, the birth of a baby or the approaching end of full-time employment and hence may be easier for the coachee to deal with compared with the externally triggered crises. It is about what we can do to discover and achieve who and what I want to be and, crucially, what life expects from me in order for me to feel fulfilled.

> **Activity**
>
> In terms of The Balanced Life, how would you describe your current state of balance? Thinking in terms of the four quadrants (Body, Mind, Heart and Soul), are there any quadrants where the balance is less positive? If so, why? Is that the result of a conscious decision? Of matters currently beyond your control? What are the implications? Where might you be able to make commensurate compensation?

We get clues about when this might be of relevance to the coachee through listening to their choice of words:

- 'values-based' language (fairness; reciprocity; goals; need to belong or integrate; need to love and be loved; respect; control; curiosity; understanding);
- 'meaning-based' language (making a difference; putting something back; inspiration; wisdom); and
- 'spirit-based' or 'soul-based' language (identity/purpose/values; faith; Higher Power; Soul).

Sometimes the corridor of entry is clear because the coachee begins to talk about their lack of drive or passion, time or energy.[18] Then the investigation centres on what exactly is missing.

Is this preoccupation with The Balanced Life simply the proverbial 'mid-life crisis', the point in our life that Joseph Campbell once described so poignantly as being triggered when reaching the top of the ladder only to find it was against the wrong wall? Certainly there's an element of a 'stage we go through', comparable to the dramas of adolescence. The entry point is a sense that what worked before no longer seems to fit. The comfortable shoes have suddenly started to pinch. The challenge is to renew ourselves, to face a transformation that is about finding the right wall. It is reaching the precipice of The Existential Leap (see Chapter 2).

This challenge often seems to span the age groups, across genders, ignores race and strikes almost irrespective of personality-type. Here perhaps more than anywhere else the coach needs to be prepared to challenge the coachee to new thinking and to be prepared to amend both the direction and the content of the coaching even if this entails refining the original engagement goals.

The 'traditional' assumption[19] of life's unfolding has been: education ‡ training ‡ work ‡ retirement (= leisure). No one asked whether this was 'meaningful', there was little option or flexibility. But increasingly that feels hollow and unsatisfying to a growing number of people. Coaches will increasingly come across these people in the coaching context. Questions about meaning are likely to be closer to the surface over the coming years. Let me change the metaphor slightly: if our role as coaches is to leave no stone unturned in helping our coachees be the best they can, under what stones might we find these questions hiding? What stones can coaches drop on coachees' seesaws in order to challenge complacent equilibrium? While many claim not to currently have a balanced life, how will they recognise what it looks and feels like if they want to search for it?

## *Happiness, well-being and satisfaction*

Three keystones are often identified as essential components in The Balanced Life. Where these three keystones exist the result is usually greater employee well-being (whether created by self or organisation) which itself then often results in better job performance, increased motivation and commitment, less absenteeism and even more job satisfaction. These three components are happiness, well-being and satisfaction.

People who are *happy* carry their positivity with them to work, to their social and leisure activities, to their participation in voluntary activities and then they infect others. Those who are stressed at work (or elsewhere) often take that ith them and are equally infectious. Most people, if ...nged, would probably agree they'd *prefer* a goal of happiness, well-being and satisfaction.

In terms of *well-being*, there have been so many articles, talks, webcasts and interviews across the gamut of mental, physical and intellectual well-being that its importance seems widely accepted. Little needs to be said here other than perhaps to note with interest that in comparison there's been a deafening silence on the area of spiritual well-being.

People who are deeply *satisfied* are often described as having something different about them, a sense of peace or tranquillity that exists separate from and largely unaffected by external situations. Deeply satisfied people may indeed be under pressure. But the sense of peace and tranquillity remains evident both to themselves and those around them.

Each of these three terms – happiness, well-being and satisfaction – is significant because although each is an emotional state they are based on something deeper and more substantial. Without this, these emotional states are only frothy, superficial and transitory. With that deeper base, however, they are relatively permanent, powerful and transformational. In part this is a strong sense of purpose and meaning both in the present and concerning the future and their part in it. They have a sense of where they are, where they're going and why.

In 2005, business coach Stephen Shapiro (*Goal-free Living*) surveyed 1,000 Americans about goal-setting. Fifty-eight per cent said they were consciously sacrificing today's happiness in order that achieving their goals would bring fulfilment. However, 41 per cent also acknowledged that when they did achieve their goals this brought little or no satisfaction, condemning them to a perpetual cycle of sacrifice, striving, disappointment and ultimately disillusionment. It appears that many crave happiness, well-being and satisfaction but have little idea where they can be found. They certainly aren't found where we've been led to believe. The corridors lead to rooms; but when we get there they're not furnished with what we were looking for, no matter how ornate or expensive.

## *Signature strengths*

This raises the question of whether these essential components of The Balanced Life are encountered by chance or whether they can be proactively seized and developed. Martin Seligman,[20] the founder of the positive psychology movement, argued that three specific elements need to be proactively built into our daily existence: the Pleasant Life; the Good Life; and the Meaningful Life. *The Pleasant Life* usually refers to things like food, shopping, watching television, etc. There is nothing wrong with these, we all need them; but while they make us happy in the short term they are ultimately unsatisfying (in Herzberg's terminology), resulting in the constant need to replenish and upscale yet destined to never fully satisfy (not unlike a craving or an addiction). *The Good Life*, 'knowing yourself and truly being yourself', depends on the ability to discover and regularly exercise those things we're really good at. (Seligman calls these 'signature strengths' and has identified 24.) The hard part is committing to actually use these signature strengths consciously and frequently in each quadrant and dimension of our life.

Using our signature strengths daily provides us with a more sustaining happiness But if using our signature strengths consciously and frequently provides *us* with happiness, proactively and deliberately using them to help *others* via The Meaningful Life produces the most-sustained happiness and the greatest sense of well-being. *The Meaningful Life* is simultaneously both the least-used and the most significant. It is, in effect, the recognition that not only is each person connected to every other person but that this web of connectivity draws us into a sense of corporate responsibility.

Point 6: *The first challenge of The Balanced Life is to help coachees find their individual combination in each of the quadrants that will produce the most-sustaining happiness and sense of well-being, to be the best of who they are both for themselves and for those around them: The Meaningful Life.*

Recently, and especially in some of the new generations entering work, these fundamental questions are already being asked and especially expressed in terms of challenging why leisure, for example, must be postponed until retirement and why there cannot be overlap between the different segments. And these very same people are asking fundamental questions of employers around their ethical and corporate social responsibility and an expectation that their own desire for meaning at work be recognised. A profoundly different approach to 'work-life balance' is emerging. This means that for us as coaches, we can increasingly expect to be taken into those areas as more of our coachees seek to explore them. Certainly, Generation X (born mid-60s to the end of the 70s) often exhibit a rejection of postponed gratification and a significantly higher expectation of what employers and other groups will provide for them. There are emerging signs that members of Generation Y (born 1980–2000) are beginning to ask even more searching questions about what constitutes a Balanced Life. Enter the next phase...

## Part 3: The expression of spirituality

Susan Jeffers expressed it like this in her book *Feel the Fear And Do It Anyway*:

> It's about moving to the strongest, most loving part of who I am. That to me is a spiritual process. It's to live as much as you can in the realm of the Higher Self, the best of who you are ... tuning into the energy that draws you to what is best for your life.[21]

There is a resurgence of people interested in questions of spirituality (though not necessarily of religion). The areas of Faith Development (see Fowler in Chapter 7) and of Spiritual Intelligence (see Wigglesworth in Chapters 2, 6 and 7) are becoming particularly important tools for coaches. A key corridor question to ask coachees might be: 'What do you *really* dream of becoming?'

The inward quest to be the best we can, the tuning in for and responding to the energy from the Higher Self is not necessarily just self-indulgence. It has much wider implications. It leads to challenging not only ourselves but also those around us. And in terms of seeking The Balanced Life that inevitably challenges long-established assumptions in each element of life, including work, and especially then how we choose to allocate our precious and limited time. Often the assumption (and perhaps fear) is that redressing an impoverished Balanced Life will demand dramatic change and probably sacrifice. We think of the merchant banker driven to become a teacher; the entrepreneur who abandons all for an African village; the marketing guru now happily market gardening. But does that really mean the only way to a balanced life is to abandon the 'rat-race'? Often this is not the case. But the requirement is a willingness to risk The Existential Leap, to begin stripping away the layers. The image is the onion: not just in the commonly used sense of peeling back the layers but because, having peeled back the layers, what lies at the core is a shoot – new growth needing to be set free to flourish and grow. That growth draws on the nurturing of the Higher Power.

For this reason alone the quadrant of spirituality should not be ignored. Of course, not every coachee will be ready or willing to explore the 'spiritual' dimension but it is important for coaches to *offer* the opportunity and the skills to pursue it. If the offer is accepted: the rewards for the coachee are significant.

### Activity

(This activity is based on a created case study.)

Andy is in his early forties. As a publisher he's had several major successes finding new writers whose books, as well as gaining high readership, have translated into moderately successful films. The publishing company, an international force to be reckoned with, rates him highly. The arrangement also gives Andy the opportunity to pursue his sporting passion, a lifelong love of basketball. At 6' 3", he'd been a successful amateur but never near professional standard. And now as he settles down with a young family and a mortgage debt that would have brought tears to the eyes of his parents his burgeoning success is matched by his burgeoning waistline. It is indeed, as he had recently remarked to his wife, 'a pleasant life'.

Enter Juanita, longstanding friend of both Andy and his wife Cassy. Juanita reckons that one of the perks of being a longstanding friend is the right to take them down a peg or two if they get too caught up with themselves; to challenge complacency when she sees it. And she reckons Andy has it in shedloads. A supper party presents the perfect opportunity.

'So, Andy, another published book in the Top 25 Titles, eh? Congratulations.' No hint of the impending bullet.

'Yep. I guess I must be lucky,' he grins. 'Certainly doesn't do any harm to my reputation with my boss.' Cassy also grins, pleased for her husband, though perhaps only after the slightest of hesitations.

Juanita raises her wine glass. 'So – what's next in this glittering mega-career?' Her victim remains blissfully unaware as, like a lion stalking its prey, she slowly moves in.

'Oh, I don't know. More of the same, I guess. And we're planning a home cinema room in a few months, bonuses permitting.'

'Home cinema room? Wow.' Her eyebrows arch. 'Impressive. What else is on the cards?' The trap is tightening.

'We're thinking of taking the kids to South America next year for a month. Help them experience another culture firsthand. And we're thinking about a new kitchen, even an extension. Oh, and Cassy's car's nearing three years old, so we need to build that in as well . . . I'll probably be looking for some promotion after all that!' And still he can't feel the breath of the predator closing in . . .

'My, quite the little empire-builder, aren't we?' Crash! Juanita knows perfectly well that 'empire-builders' was what Andy had used at university as a derogatory condemnation of materialism, complacency and superficiality.

Now Andy has felt the claws. And they've sunk deep, momentarily paralysing. Cassy is watching with fascination: she knows exactly where this is leading. And to her surprise, she finds herself very much favouring Juanita. 'Go, girl,' she mutters.

'So this is Andy mid-term, then? Your destiny summed up as a home cinema, new car and an educational trip to the Amazon jungle . . . That's how you define yourself, you who 20 years ago was destined to change the world?' Ouch. With clinical precision, she's gone for the jugular.

> Several days later Andy is at a scheduled meeting with you as his coach. He's relayed the story to you and acknowledged that it has actually quite shaken him, especially the bit about 'empire-building'. Identify some key 'coaching' questions to ask in order to find out about possible causes. (This is the 'R' part of the GROW Coaching Model. See Chapter 6 if you are unfamiliar with the model.)
>
> The process here is rather like the earlier onion-peeling metaphor: the peeled-back conversation might go through numerous layers before it reaches the core, the seed of what is really going on.[22] And there are no right or wrong answers. As an example, let's start here: 'What was it about Juanita's conversation that "brought you up short", as you put it?'
>
> 'I guess, need to look again at how I'm spending my time. Far too long at work. Need to – want to – spend more family time.'
>
> As a coach, you might keep in mind the section above about the Meaningful Life: knowing yourself and truly being yourself, and perhaps frame some questions using them. The idea of signature strengths (proactively using our signature strengths daily which results in sustaining happiness) might be useful for Andy.
>
> Later in this coaching session Andy has acknowledged that: 'The "meaning" part was helpful – I can understand what you're getting at. But I still feel there's more to it . . . Probably because Juanita reminded me I used to bore everyone, going on about a real sense of calling and destiny.'
>
> Frame where you might pursue this next in the context of broadening Andy's understanding and exploration, especially into 'spirituality'. There are some possible questions in Chapter 7.

For Andy at this point there has been progression through three layers of the onion, as it were. Layer 1 was about finding a balanced life (time and priority management); Layer 2 was about a search for meaning (a need to make sense); Layer 3 was entering the realm of spirituality (a need to find purpose and fulfil his destiny, his calling).

In Chapter 2 I introduced the idea of The Existential Leap, that point in life marking a radical reassessment of who we are and what we want to be and do, the sense of teetering on the brink of something new and challenging. It is the point at which we recognise not so much our individuality as our interconnectedness. It is also the realisation of an external calling and the ensuing implications for who we are, what we do, why we do it and who we do it for and with. I suggested that it might be part of the proverbial 'mid-life crisis'. Without in any way denying that, I want to also suggest that for an increasing number of people, perhaps a whole generation, those questions are being asked much earlier, at a sort of 'quarter-life crisis'.[23] Issues of The Balanced Life are no longer the sole preserve (or soul-preserve) of advancing years.

The story of Richard Purchase (Box 3.1) describes this Existential Leap in terms of The Balanced Life.

### Box 3.1 Richard Purchase

It was something of a mid-career crisis – or at least reappraisal – that led Richard to fundamentally challenge his balance between 'work' and 'life'. As a trained pharmacist in both Bermuda and the English NHS he had been invited back into the pharmaceutical industry to head sales teams and for 'nine really good years, worked with hugely impressive leaders' and was on the UK board.

But having reached board level and still not exactly even 'mid' career, he was wondering what to do next. This forced him to reconsider two things:

- To what extent was he currently operating his core values?
- What was it he wanted to *get from* his work and what was it he wanted to *give to* it?

Recognising that helping others and team-working were key parts of both his work ethos and his recreation (he is a hockey coach and former international player), he wanted something that gave him a chance to put something back, to make a difference to other people's lives, while at the same time enabling him to spend more time outside work.

> The key moment was looking back at the times when he'd felt most fulfilled and complete – 'to be happy waking up and looking at myself in the mirror' – which had happened when he was involved in work that made a difference, in education and also in the NHS.
>
> This led him to become managing director of a private-sector group involved in the education sector, where he soon became involved in setting up academies. In June 2008 he was headhunted to the Alpha Plus group, where his role is to grow the group and get in place the right structures for economic growth. *'We have a very clear sense of purpose, total focus on children and what we do for them and for parents. We need to focus on getting the best possible people for the job, then look after them.'*
>
> Your funeral oration?
>
> He was a good man, he cared, he was quite special in the way he touched the lives of others.
>
> *'The times when I've felt most effective and fulfilled in leadership have been when I've had a significant car commute – often up to two hours. It's been a time for processing and reflection. I miss the time for peace and meditation, for the positive visualisation of scoring the goal.'* As such, he values the Buddhist Eightfold Path and its sense of reflection and meditation in order to restore his priorities.

## *'Right Roads' and the 'Dark Woods'*

While there may be as many roads into the exploration of spirituality in The Balanced Life as there are people there are also some common signposts. Signpost *questions* might include:

- If friends phoned tonight to come and stay – how long would it be before you could fit them in?
- Does it matter to you? Why?
- If the whole of your diary were suddenly cleared of work for the next week only – what would you choose to do instead?

- Surely there must be more to life than this? (However flippantly it's said.)

Signpost *events* are rather more obvious clues: childbirth; marriage or a civil partnership; impending retirement, etc.

What one sees at the precipice-edge in looking round and looking backwards and looking forwards depends on where that person is in their life stages; on their personality; and on their life-experiences to date. And perhaps it also depends on what they feel they have to lose if the leap is unsuccessful: the attraction of the future versus the allure of the past.

This moment of suddenly awakening teetering on the edge of the precipice is graphically described in Dante's (midlife) conundrum when he awoke to find himself in a dark wood, all traces of familiarity and 'right' pathways vanished.

In themselves, these questions and events are neither Dark Woods nor Right Roads. But perception is everything and the life re-assessment and re-adjustment events can potentially cloud the brightest sun, to mix metaphors. Certainly they have the potential to awaken afresh the recognition of something or someone greater 'out there', a re-examination of who we are, what we do and why we do it, a renewed commitment to the greater good and of 'life is about more than this'.

## *Spiritual Intelligence and The Balanced Life*

In my experience, coaches are more likely to be asking questions about spirituality and their legacy when considering 'work-life balance' than, for example, in considering the next step in their career progression.

There is emerging evidence to suggest that there are stages in *spiritual* development just as there are within the other intelligences (intellectual, physical and emotional). With Andy in the previous case study, it was at a very preliminary emergent state and his coach would need to be a skilled 'midwife' if the baby is to be delivered safely and flourish. The good news is that, with exercise, feeding and care, SQ (Spiritual Intelligence) can grow at least as fast as its sibling intelligences. If coaches understand these different developmental stages, their role will be much more effective.

This suggests that the coachee may be asking different questions and seeking different answers in the 'Spirit' quadrant to those in the 'Mind' or 'Heart' ones (see Figure 3.1 above).

> **Activity**
>
> 1. What are the issues and questions of The Balanced Life relevant to each quadrant (of Body, Mind, Heart and Soul) especially concerning Time Sovereignty;[24] happiness, well-being and satisfaction?
> 2. Using the Jeffers quote at the beginning of this section, ask the coachee: 'If you had now reached the point of achieving this, what would you be doing?' Then ask, 'How might you get there?'

The coach will need to tailor the sophistication of their questions to the SQ level of their coachee. This is covered in more detail in Chapter 5. The good news is that as coaches we don't need to be *experts* in these stages of development. It is important to be familiar with their *existence*, to have a broad overview and to recognise that the people we coach will be at different stages that will affect what triggers their questioning about *The Balanced Life* – and probably what answers they find satisfying. But fundamentally our role is simply to accompany them and maybe even learn alongside them.

## *Energy*

Exercising Body, Mind and Heart has a widely recognised side-benefit: the generation of energy! A plethora of articles deal with the importance of fully developing physically, mentally and emotionally. But less attention has been paid to spiritual energy: what Schwartz and McCarthy describe as 'energy of meaning and purpose'.[25] Yet its importance is highlighted by one piece of recent research quoted in the *Harvard Business Review*,[26] which notes that while 'time' spent is gone, 'energy' spent is renewable and helps build physical, emotional, mental *and spiritual* energy (emphasis mine).

Energy, passion and spirit are intertwined and replenishing one is crucial to replenishing the other. The soul, the 'location' of the spirit, is like a nuclear reactor's core, the generator of the energy. To tackle just the other areas, however prominent they are, is to tackle the symptoms rather than the cause, like repeatedly changing blown electrical fuses rather than rewiring the house.

So energy is a vital component of spirituality. One of the most common complaints by those who feel their life to be out of balance is their ensuing lack of energy. Energy (in terms of SQ) is generated and renewed by 'sweet spot' activities, things we find absorbing, fascinating, engrossing and enjoy the most. They are also generally activities that take us outside ourselves and foster a broader understanding, empathy and engagement. This might involve no more than a quiet contemplation of the natural landscape during a break between meetings in order to enjoy our place in the world we inhabit. Or it might be the lasting buzz we feel from seeing someone really helped and changed by a voluntary activity in which we participated. Or responding to our sense of being called to give something back. These activities are food for the soul. Indeed this latter form of energy is the most dynamic, the most sustaining, the most deeply satisfying and the most enduring. All of which points to the importance of coaches helping coachees recognise both those things that replenish their spiritual energy – and those that leech it away.

### Activity

What can coaches do to help coachees identify and adopt their 'sweet spot' activities across each dimension of their life? What are the potential leeches? Where do they come from and how might they be repelled?

Perhaps the underpinning metaphor of this chapter is the engine of a motor car: where all the cogs and parts are present, in tune and interacting, there is smooth performance and energy generation; where one or more of them is out of balance the whole vehicle can feel juddery and lacking in power.

## Summary

*The Balanced Life* rarely means complete equilibrium. It is also not constant but varies at different times of life, in different circumstances, sometimes even from day to day. But it is about being in tune, both internally and externally. That means recognising and developing each dimension of our lives and especially the energy-generating area of spirituality in order to navigate through the dark woods in our search for our right road.

One final story to finish this chapter:

### Box 3.2

A group of business graduates were meeting for a reunion at the home of one of their professors. Pretty soon the conversation got round to their current jobs and one after the other complained of their unsatisfactory work-life balance, the stress they felt, the pressure they were under. The professor left the room to make the coffee.

When he returned with the coffee pot the tray was laden with an assortment of cups and mugs ranging from the typical student-chipped to the obviously-expensive porcelain. He offered round the drinks.

Once each had their drink the professor called the meeting to order. 'You have each gone for the best cup available to you, even enviously eying those around you to see if anyone has a better cup than you. Yet the cup adds nothing to the coffee, it is merely a tool to hold it. The type of cup we're given in life doesn't define the quality of the life we live. Sometimes by over-concentrating on the cup we fail to enjoy the coffee.'[27]

## Part 4: Further activities

*The Rainbow Years* has a very useful exercise around the question, 'How spiritual am I?' (Hopson and Scally, 2008, Activities 7.1 and 7.2, p. 161). It also contains some valuable insights into The Balanced Life.

### *Activity 1*

Shakespeare famously reminded us of our lifespan of 'three-score years and ten'; nowadays, we might more realistically move towards imagining it as four-score and ten! Using an image such as a torch battery or a fuel tank, how much of the battery energy do I feel I've consumed? Do I feel it's been spent wisely? How much is left? How might I top it up? How might I now choose to use the energy?

### *Activity 2*

Start with the question, 'What's really important to *me*?' List the top 10. But now imagine the infamous hot-air balloon exercise where the balloon basket is overweight and ballast must be discarded. Which five would you discard? Finally, in order to really fly again, it's down to three. What are they?

Next, if I'm really 'flying' (i.e. living the life I really want to be living, making the fullest use of those three things that are so very important to me), what does that look like? Feel like? What changes do I need to make in order to achieve this? And over what timescale? What might prevent me and how might I avoid the barriers?

### *Activity 3*

On a day-to-day basis, how do I know when I'm in balance? What am I doing? What am I not doing?

### *Activity 4*

Ask individual coachees or groups, 'What do you think are the universal values?' The answers of course are less important than the language used and the ensuing debate.

## Activity 5

The Life Balance Wheel: Make a list of between 6 and 10 components that, for you, make up your life. They might include work, dreams/aspirations, physical health, family relationships, friends, relationships, faith involvement, recreation activities, financial, etc. Then draw a wheel with each item scattered around the outer rim. Connect each into the centre with a dotted line. If the centre of the circle, the inner hub, represents 0 per cent and the outer rim 100 per cent, mark your current level of satisfaction for each component. What does the shape of your life look like? What would you like it to look like? (Really?)

## Activity 6

Draw four columns downwards on a piece of paper. List the main events of the past couple of weeks down the page in the first column. In the second column, alongside each event, describe what your function was, e.g. planning, leading, negotiating, just being there ... In the third column, note whether this was work, recreation, personal, social, etc. In the final column, in terms of energy or sense of fulfilment and achievement, would it rate as a positive (+) or a negative (–)? What do you notice? Is there a strong bias in a particular area? Which of your core values are represented – or missing? Anything else noticeably missing? Any changes needed?

## Activity 7

Rank the following statements in terms of *very important*; *important*; *quite important*; *not important*. (Coaches: Remember that these are conversation-prompts. There is no right or wrong answer or interpretation: if your coachee asks what it means, it literally does mean whatever they would like it to mean!) For example, if 'doing things better than they've ever been done before' is one of your main drivers, a constant feature of what motivates you and spurs you on, then you will probably rate it *very important*.

## *Work*

- Doing things better than they've ever been done before.
- Being recognised for my contribution in developing other people.
- Being liked by the people I work with.
- The opportunity to work in collaboration and co-operation with others.
- I try to minimise conflict.
- People think of me as a sympathetic listener.
- I need to interact with other people at work.
- Doing things that make things better for other people.
- I value having a peaceful place for reflection.
- Where there is a choice, I put the needs of others before my own.
- Work that enables me to be a positive influence in people's lives.
- I seek work that gives me influence/power to change things.
- When someone asks me what I do, I am proud because I feel I make a real difference.
- There must be more to life than this.
- Work to live – or live to work?
- Working for an organisation with clear and positive business ethics.
- I like to feel that my work is contributing to society.
- Working for an organisation that somehow contributes to a better society.

## *Personal, social and family*

- Having plenty of time at the present to spend with friends.
- Having plenty of time currently to spend with family.
- Having sufficient time currently to devote to all the social activities I want to pursue.
- Earning enough money to support my family's standard of living at the level we aspire to.

Finally . . .

- What are you passionate about?
- Where do you spend your discretionary effort?

- What are your dreams, the things you'd do if you won the lottery?
- When time flies – what are you doing?
- My key learning from this is . . .
- As a result, I intend to . . .

## *Activity 8*

- What is a life well lived?
- What would you like more of in your life?

## *Activity 9*

Learn your 3x tables!

- 3 times when you felt fulfilled?
- 3 times you when you felt most valued?

   1.
   2.
   3.

- Your 3 best skills or qualities as identified by others?

   1.
   2.
   3.

## *Activity 10*

*Hindsight in advance technique*: imagine we are sitting in this room one year from now (give date, time, etc.). We are looking back over the year. In your deepest levels of honesty, what excuses might you have (one year from now) for not achieving some of the goals we've talked about today? Identify several, especially those over which you could have had control.

- When you say (e.g.), 'I didn't take the tough decisions I might have done', what do you have in mind?
- What stopped you making those 'tough decisions'?

- So coming back to today (specify date and time), what actions do you now need to take in order to prepare for taking those 'tough decisions' when they arrive?

## *Activity 11*

Charles Handy[28] has suggested that motivation is created through a series of words, each beginning with 'E', with the first, 'Effort', occupying disproportionate attention! This chart (Table 3.1) invites you to shade as a barometer your current level for each of his 'E' terms.

What does this say about your current balance? About nurturing your spirit (or soul)?

## *Activity 12*

Using the four quadrants of Heart, Mind, Soul and Spirit, consider which are under-catered, which over-catered and which you feel are in balance. What are the implications?

## *Activity 13*

Deepak Chopra argues that gratitude is one of the most effective ways of getting in touch with our soul. 'When you're in touch with your soul, you eavesdrop on the wisdom of the universe.' What is your reaction to these words?

## *Activity 14*

Which, if any, of the following comments might have come from your mouth?

- 'I don't invest enough time and energy in making a positive difference to others or to the world.'
- 'There are significant gaps between what I say is most important to me in my life and how I actually allocate my time and energy.'
- 'My decisions at work are more often influenced by external demands than by a strong, clear sense of my own purpose.'

Table 3.1 The barometer of motivation

| 100 per cent | | | | | | |
|---|---|---|---|---|---|---|
| 90 | | | | | | |
| 80 | | | | | | |
| 70 | | | | | | |
| 60 | | | | | | |
| 50 | | | | | | |
| 40 | | | | | | |
| 30 | | | | | | |
| 20 | | | | | | |
| 10 | | | | | | |
| 0 | | | | | | |
| | Energy | Excitement | Enthusiasm | Emotion | Expenditure of TIME | Expenditure of MONEY | Expenditure of PASSION |

## *Activity 15*

'What accomplishment am I most proud of?' or 'What in my life am I happy about?'

There is some useful information about work-life balance on the Investors in People website: www.investorsinpeople.co.uk

# 4

# Spirituality and crises

**Overview**

In the previous chapter, I talked about the struggles for and benefits of achieving work-life balance, The Balanced Life. I made the point that those issues are often encountered at the moment when we suddenly, dramatically, awake from a dream and find ourselves at the precipice-edge of The Existential Leap. Although the corridors of approach and the dark woods of that moment often are (or feel) beyond out control, how we respond is largely within our own control; looking around and the choice of whether to leap or not is largely under own control. And the more control we feel we have, the lower our levels of stress and the higher the levels of satisfaction, happiness and well-being. I argued that while The Balanced Life was relevant to all four quadrants of Body, Mind, Heart and Spirit it was particularly applicable to the latter two because there the focus shifts from self to others. There appears to be a close correlation between a sense of helping others and being drawn to fulfilling one's sense of calling, leaving a legacy and the sense of happiness, well-being and satisfaction that signal a balanced life.

But there are times when we are literally hit by the unexpected with the force of an express train. These are the times of real crises far more shattering and profound than those that are often dubbed 'crises' by an over-sensationalising media. With crises, we are often hurtled not just to the edge of the precipice but catapulted beyond, far beyond. One of the defining features of crisis is the feeling of complete loss of control. Welcome to the crisis. Its presence is well documented by shell-shocked writers, painters and diarists across the centuries. Dante wrote hauntingly of suddenly awaking in a dark wood with all traces of familiarity erased.

Many will recognise crises that have heralded the dark woods of Dante's conundrum. Many can identify moments or even large swathes of their life in the dark wood where the 'right road' felt wholly lost. Sometimes those events may be self-induced, sometimes utterly beyond their control. Sometimes they are individual (such as a struggle with alcoholism or redundancy); sometimes they may involve the immediate small group (such as a family bereavement); and occasionally they may have a far wider embrace (the closing of a town's main employer, or the outbreak of animal infectious disease in a farming region, or even a terrorist attack). The approach and dawning of a new millennium fostered much debate about whether we were on the right road and about what sort of society was desired for the twenty-first century, much as two world wars had done in the last century of the previous millennium.

### Box 4.1 The boy and the cloth bag

A small boy had a prized possession – a large cloth bag. Everywhere he went he carried it with him. Every time someone said something that made him cry or stung him, he drew the sting out from his heart and dropped it into his bag. Every action that he associated with pain, everything he wanted to ward off, was deflected into it. Once in the bag it protected him from hearing or feeling those harsh words and unkind actions again. And he added to it those desires from his own thoughts and heart that others criticised or discouraged, those bits of himself that didn't fit the mould others were expecting him to fill.

Over the years as the boy grew bigger so did the bag. More and more went into it. But the boy didn't seem to notice. After all, it grew as he grew and just became part of his life. And carrying it meant that he was able to become the person that others wanted to see. He grew with their approvals and their

> expectations; and he put behind him all those things that earned their disapproval.
>
> The boy grew into a youth and for a while the bag seemed sealed. Nothing went into it. In fact he took great pride in the fact that the bag was sealed and that he was now the person he wanted to be.
>
> Life progressed. He got his first career step. He married. He looked at his life as it stretched ahead of him. And he felt contented. Once or twice he was even tempted to leave the bag behind. But whenever he did, he missed its familiarity, he felt incomplete. So he would pick it up again, reasoning, 'I'm my own person. I'm not deflecting things into it any more. There's no harm in carrying it with me.' And he heaved it back onto his shoulder.
>
> One day about the time of his thirtieth birthday his own baby was born — a son. It was as he looked into the still-unseeing eyes of the newborn, as he considered what he wanted for his own son, that once more he became aware of the weight of the sack he carried.
>
> But this time he really was aware of the weight, the enormity of it. And as he became aware of its enormity he also knew for a blinding certainty that he did not want his own son to carry such a burden. He wanted only the best for him. Henceforth this would be his top priority, his greatest commitment. At that same moment, unseen, a tiny bag appeared behind the infant's back . . .[1]

This brief but vitally important chapter looks at baggage picked up over the years and the crises that may provide gateway opportunities leading to The Existential Leap, the re-examination of meaning and spirituality.

Part of the reason this is a short chapter is because dealing with crises and their aftermath is often not within either the remit or the expertise of the coach. Coaching is not the same as either counselling or therapy and it is vital that coaches and coachees recognise and maintain the distinct boundaries. Some coaches may indeed be trained as therapists; but even then (or perhaps especially then), the coachee/client must be transparently clear about what they are getting and the coach about what they are providing. It must be explicit, not assumed. There is a fundamental question about when to refer the coachee on to a specialist and to whom. Many coaches will have contacts and recommendations; professional associations likewise. Coaching supervisors provide an additional point of reference.

## Part 1: Crises

What is a crisis? When is a crisis not a crisis but merely an uncomfortable ripple in the tide of life? Perhaps the simplest way to define it is by the response it elicits. A deep crisis challenges our assumptions, throws up into the air everything we hold dear and had assumed to be not only true but also permanent. And usually it occurs as result of something that we have not chosen. So it is hardly surprising that crises such as a relationship breakup often result in the raising of our eyes and thoughts to things that lie beyond and above the everyday, an increased awareness of spirituality as a potential source of stability in the eye of the storm.

There are three different types of crises to consider here: universal crises; culturally specific crises; and life cycle crises.

### *Universal crises*

These are experienced by almost everyone at some time or other, irrespective of who we are or where we live. For example:

- Breakup of significant relationships.
- Bereavement.
- Facing our own mortality.
- Facing our own death.

While we may draw some comfort that everyone else is likely to go through these at some time or other, often several times, that neither diminishes the power nor the impact on fundamental reappraisal. There is also a certain commonality of response across cultures and continents. I'm referring to the private emotional reaction to them rather than the collective rituals of the public response, although the way in which they are handled publically may be a major factor in the scale of impact.

## *Culturally specific crises*

With these the reaction might differ according to where we live. These might include:

- Redundancy.
- Illness.
- War and acts of terrorism (e.g. Twin Towers).
- The unfolding of history around us (e.g. the new millennium).

Again, there may be comfort in the commonality of the experience but often the responses triggered by these crises can only be faced once the events themselves have passed and been internalised. And that response can vary widely from one individual to another, sometimes diametrically. For example, one person caught up in the trauma of the Twin Towers explosions considers it proof of the futility of belief in any kind of Higher Power; another, proof of that very existence. One person faces their imminent death with magnanimity and peace, another with alcohol-fuelled denial.

## *Life-cycle crises*

These are events that a culture assumes to be part of the 'natural' cycle of life but that nevertheless trigger a fundamental re-appraisal:

- Approaching retirement and a drive to consider 'legacy'.
- Retirement itself – or lack of it as an option.
- Empty Nest Syndrome.[2]

Sometimes the perceived trauma of an approaching new life stage, of simply progressing our lives, precipitates a new consideration, a process of re-framing may already have begun. 'Does the process of spiritual development itself invite greater choice regarding how we emotionally and spiritually relate to and establish boundaries around one another and hence precipitate potential crises?' ponders the American business coach Cindy Wigglesworth.[3]

One of the most prominent life cycle elements in Western society, even winning itself a cliché-label, is the mid-life crisis, commonly attached to any mildly uncharacteristic behaviour occurring anytime between the ages of about 35–55. As I said previously, it was memorably described by the writer Joseph Campbell as being the moment in life when you reach the top of the ladder only to find that it is against the wrong wall. Several decades of effort and dedication suddenly feels misplaced, the achievements hollow and the gains superficial.

Key questions in each of these three types of crisis often find articulation via words associated with dreams, idealism, transformation and legacy.

## Part 2: The coaching implications

A common feature of each of these types of crisis is that explanations and patterns of behaviour that worked before are unlikely to work now: life itself seems to demand that we change, adapt and grow if we are to remain healthy. These crises really do lead us to the edge of The Existential Leap and beyond and challenge us to jump into the unknown or at least the dimly discerned. The Existential Leap commonly challenges us to rephrase the previous primary driver, 'What do I want?' with a new one: 'What is being called *from* me?'

One of the features of 'coaching for meaning and spirituality' with people in crisis is their constantly shifting goals as needs and focuses evolve. By definition crises are times of flux, uncertainty and re-examination, so it's hardly surprising that those caught up in their tentacles see their perceptions and perspectives frequently change. It is important for the coach to demonstrate flexibility and to regularly check whether the coachee's goals have changed, and if so, how and to what. This is a time of turbulence, of storm, of constantly shifting sandstorms of emotion almost on a daily basis. It is also a journey not being undertaken alone.

Typical gateway language at this initial point will tend to focus around confusion and uncertainty:

- Is this it?
- Why? Why did this happen? Why to me? To them?
- This hasn't happened.
- It all seems beyond me to cope with.

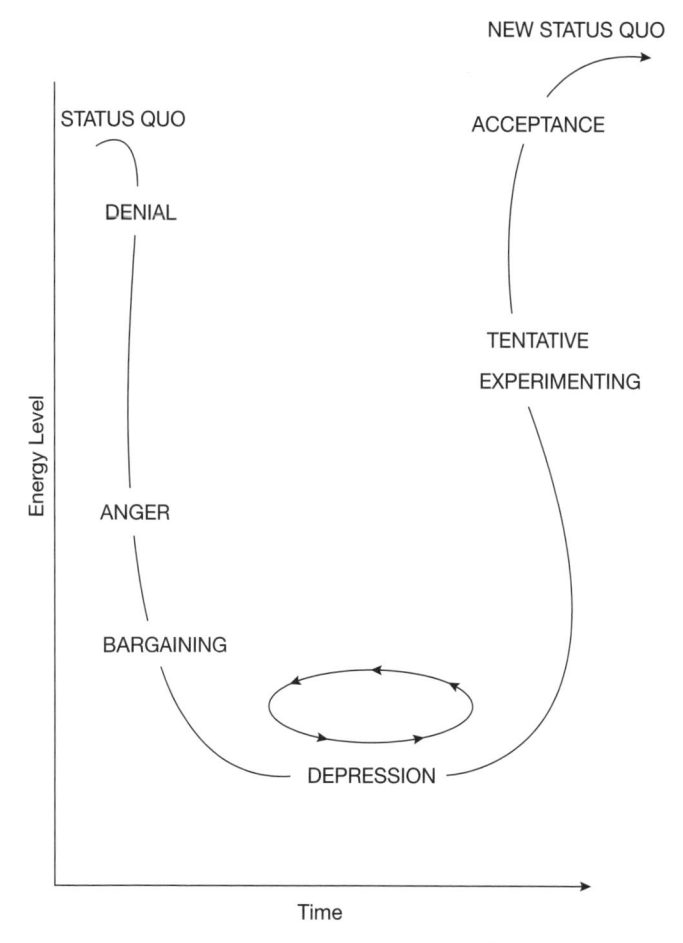

*Figure 4.1* **Energy level and time**

These are, of course, classic post-trauma stages:[4] denial, anger, bargaining, depression, tentative acceptance and acceptance leading to the new status quo.

Often the next stage will include wanting to move into something richer, broader and potentially more fulfilling; seeking opportunities for greater self-expression; moving from head to heart/soul living.

Of course, not everyone is willing to undertake this and the coach may need to pull back. Or they may be unable to undertake it: the issue seems too powerful, too deep-rooted or intransigent so that the coach may need to suggest specialist counselling. As a very rough rule-of-thumb, there are four things that might indicate this point of referral has been reached:

1. Time/Proximity. It is my belief that coaching is rarely appropriate significantly close to the precipitating crisis as emotions may be especially raw.
2. Intensity/Dislocation. Again, this is a matter of degree, with the greater the impact of the crisis the less likely it is for coaching to be appropriate.
3. Response/Reaction to the coaching process – again, a matter of degree.
4. The coach themselves sits there wondering where to go next and feeling out of their depth!

For the remainder of this chapter on crises, having drawn attention to the potential danger of coaches trespassing into territory they are neither equipped for nor mandated to enter, I shall assume that coaching has been deemed the most appropriate road for exploring those dark woods.

Coaching questions here will often revolve around the hypothetical since these are designed to help the other person step outside and away from the present moment, for example:

- 'When you look back at this time, what positives would you have liked to have drawn from it?'
- 'Suppose you had a complete free choice of action at this time, what would you do? What would you not do?'
- 'If this were happening to someone else, what would you suggest they consider?'
- 'What advice might you give yourself?'

Crises generally prompt the development of new or significantly different ways of responding, especially when previous ways of thinking have proven insufficient to deal with the current crisis. Each new stage of emotional development – sequentially – helps deal with problems that the previous stage could not. (This is true of all the intelligences.)

The ability to explore issues of meaning and spirituality probably does not require the coachee to have achieved a certain prerequisite competence or development stage in Emotional (or Intellectual) Intelligence. Some researchers such as Grant (1983) or Duniho (1991) suggest it might. But in my experience greater significance might be attached to:

- Encountering a sufficiently profound or shattering trigger event.
- The presence of a wise, supportive and challenging companion skilled for the journey.

There is little doubt that for those moving through the stages portrayed in Figure 4.1 the presence of a companion significantly enhances the ability to reflect at each stage and hence potentially move through it more quickly or at least more effectively. It also tends to lessen the likelihood of swirling around ineffectually in the quagmire of depression. The questions that coaches need to ask will be different depending on such considerations as whether the trigger is one of the universal crises (see above), one of the culturally specific crises or one of the life-cycle crises. They will also be different for different people and for people at different stages portrayed in Figure 4.1 and/or people whose current preference is to operate predominantly in a particular quadrant of the multiple intelligences. For example, 'What does this mean?' to a baby constitutes 'How do I make this part of my body work?' (PQ – Physical Quotient). To a 10 year-old it constitutes an attempt to make reasoned connections (IQ – Intelligence Quotient). To a hormone-raved teenager suddenly weak-kneed in the presence of someone special it has an entirely different arena (EQ – Emotional Quotient). And to the explorer drawing breath on the brink of The Existential Leap perhaps it means something else entirely (SQ – Spiritual Quotient).

But fundamentally the extent to which a person is able to re-assemble meaning and sense of purpose after a crisis doesn't seem to *depend* on either the trigger cause or the level of their physical, intellectual or emotional development so much as on a willingness to embrace the struggle and challenge of their paradigms. Having the right person with whom to do this makes 'successful' completion much more likely.

Thus the most transformational role of the coach is to encourage exploration by wise questioning that prompts fresh insights and understanding. To pick up Dante's dark wood analogy, there is a two-stage process.

Stage 1 is to help the coachee actually share in the darkness, to feel it, to listen to it, to reflect on it. There is a great temptation in our Western society to try to avoid pain and discomfort; but these can be times of great insight and learning for those sufficiently brave to accept the challenge. The coach may need to probe with tact and sensitivity. It's often said that the presenting issue is rarely the real issue. The Reality stage of the GROW model (see Chapter 6) is particularly useful for this and can richly repay the significant time spent on it, though too often it is only superficially visited in the drive to move on and create Options that characterise the next stage in the GROW model.[5]

Stage 2 is to facilitate the preliminary exploration of a number of different roads forward until some clarity begins to merge from the darkness, to help the coachee try to find what *feels* right, the path along which they feel called or attracted (and why). Sometimes it can be necessary for the coach to challenge the very concept of a 'right' road with its implication that every other road is somehow therefore 'wrong'. Very often the learning and insights come from the exploration and travelling, whichever road they choose, rather than remaining immobilised in case the choice proves to be the wrong one.

The next case study example (Box 4.2, names changed to preserve anonymity) illustrates the value of having a good coach available in the dark wood. People in the midst of crises often describe feeling buffeted, being blown off course or feeling all at sea: the crisis has broken them away from the safety of their moorings without the grounding of an anchor.

The coach facilitated a key phrase: 'getting back in touch with my deeper destiny'; this helped the coachee use spirituality to regain lost meaning. Some gateway terms have been italicised.

> **Box 4.2 'Susan' – Director of Operations for an NHS Foundation Trust**
>
> 'After reaching a pinnacle in my previous career I was *inspired* to join the NHS. It proved to be a good move. I was motivated by what I saw, the people I worked with and what I believed I could achieve. This *spurred me on* in my career and my desire to become a chief executive. I was *driven* by the *meaning* and potential of the NHS as a system to help improve healthcare and its potential to deliver results.
>
> After seemingly being successful in various roles and progressing well with my career the relentless pressure and sustained overdrive resulted in a disconnection between my head and my emotions. I felt I had become "mechanical" in my approach, which caused a *fundamental reappraisal* of what I wanted to achieve and whether what I was doing was *really what I wanted*.
>
> In my quest to become a chief executive I mistakenly moved into an organisation that was poles apart with my values and a political hotbed. My coach helped me through a very difficult period and helped me to recognise that whilst I was what the organisation needed, it wasn't ready to change. We agreed that in order to understand what had gone wrong I would undertake a 360-degree appraisal that my coach facilitated, which proved invaluable.
>
> It took me a while to get in touch with *my deeper destiny* in the NHS: the relentless pressure and long hours resulted in me *disconnecting* with the *meaning* of the NHS and forgetting to recognise what I could do to *make a positive impact* for the *benefit of patients* and the services they received.'
>
> Having moved from an organisation that was at odds with her values, Susan is now a director in a successful Foundation Trust and is much clearer about all sorts of things. 'I'm resolute in what I can do to *make a phenomenal difference* for patients.'

> This change of purpose has also led to a change of aspiration: instead of focusing on personal ambition (to become a chief executive), she has refocused to becoming 'as senior as I can in *order to make the biggest difference possible* for both patients and staff'.
>
> What has been the key change? '*Connecting with who I really am* and *connecting with my destiny* – which has resulted in my seeing things completely differently.
>
> It's as if life is a jigsaw and as life progresses bits begin to fall into place, with different people we encounter or things that happen to us being key pieces in helping us see the overall design.'

## Part 3: The coach as alchemist

Probably the most commonly encountered of these crises, or at least the most commented upon, is mid-life. Whether this is actually a crisis or not will depend on many factors, not least the perspective of the recipient. Certainly it is often a time of reassessment and of dramatic change. It presents an opportunity to reflect on both what has happened so far in life *and* what's desired for the remainder. I believe this is where the services of a coach can be invaluable and life changing. Where the raw ingredients are in place and the chemistry of the relationship is strong then, as Murdoch suggests, alchemy is possible:

> the un-useful behaviours, out-of-date aspirations, negative perceptions of self and life may be burnt up at this time. The alchemy at work here offers us the possibility of becoming fully functioning people, perhaps for the first time. We may now begin to experience life from the heart and soul as well as from our heads.[6]

This is a significant phase in life not only because it offers the opportunity to take a fresh look at what has gone on before and burn off the dross but also because it offers the tantalising prospect of moving closer to innate potential as a person. By entering the realms of heart and spirit that characterise the second half of life, this begins to counter-balance the head-based dominance of the first half.

There are huge challenges here for the coach as well as the coachee. Coaches are not immune from crises either; we ourselves carry baggage on our shoulders and wounds in our hearts, like the boy at the start of this chapter. Many of these crises are there for us as well. Is it necessary for the coach to have travelled this road or climbed this ladder and encountered the wrong wall in order to help the coachee? No – though it does help! What is essential is the willingness of the coach to work in a crucible that may well be uncertain to both themselves and their client. All sorts of previously held assumptions, beliefs and expectations are challenged and the outcomes may appear at best opaque and at worst unseen to both coachee and coach. They present opportunities for transformation: to miss them is to travel down a cul-de-sac: to help coachees pursue them is potentially a gold mine for them. It takes both courage and consummate professionalism to recognise occasions when we need to step back or to avoid projecting our own pain or solution onto similar crises faced by the coachee in front of us. Supervision can help; resilience is vital.

## *Resilience*

A word about resilience in the context of alchemy. This is not the same as the traditional prescription of 'Pull yourself together' or 'Grit your teeth and get on with it'. I hope as coaches we are a little more enlightened than that. Resilience is a necessary ingredient in the process of alchemy.

Research[7] suggests resilience often exhibits three key characteristics:

1. Acceptance of reality.
2. Ability to improvise: the ability to make do with whatever is at hand.
3. Deep belief, often underpinned by strongly held values, that life is meaningful: 'resilient people build bridges from present-day hardships to a fuller, better-constructed future', Coutu claims.[8]

This latter characteristic is especially relevant here, both in terms of coaching with meaning and spirituality and in terms of dealing with crises. Coutu describes it in terms of building bridges from the present hardships to a more meaningful, 'better constructed' future.

One person who was called to demonstrate resilience in the search for meaning, in the deliberations on the precipice of The Existential Leap, is Sally Adams (Box 4.3; again, not her real name). But this resilience also provided the stimulus to resolution. For her, the crisis was precipitated by a particularly difficult work situation that made her realise her career had moulded her into being the person that others expected with the result that she felt she'd sacrificed her core values and betrayed herself. She sought answers in both the horizontal and vertical dimensions.

### Box 4.3 'Sally' – a director with a Local Authority

1. Horizontally, it entailed challenging the work culture she created for herself and her staff. 'For a long time I acted what I thought was the role of manager. But it wasn't producing the workplace that I wanted. It felt false.' This contravened a core value of *authenticity*: 'Being who you want to be and who others need you to be'. Sally believes that if you put relationships as a central focus, improved performance will follow. She realised that too many people either by choice, requirement or assumption were leaving their preferred values at the door and adopting dog-eat-dog ones at work. 'Work is real life, not just a way of earning money.' So she set about creating a culture where positive relationships were central and where 'work could be irreverent'. By the time she left, someone wrote in her card: 'One of the few people who can easily make work fun.' In practical terms this meant modelling real *trust* – another core value: 'I disclose more than most other people to my team so they get the broader picture and because I trust them to treat that wisely.' Finally, '*Recognition* is also important to develop people who are great team members, supportive of each

> other, utterly trustworthy, very competent and hence create over-achieving.'
> 2. Vertically, it was a recognition of her link not just with her staff and organisation but also far wider. An image from a James Taylor song (of a river flowing out from our heart and under our feet to connect us all*) became particularly important: the *interconnectedness* of the river was very influential.' I feel my drive for authenticity, to *be my true self*, is with this feeling of being interconnected.' If life has overall meaning, we need to be honorable and decent with ourselves and with others – and not be approving of those who don't. When you think about it, it's a *miracle* we're here at all with life, at this time, in this place, with connections to these people. It's an amazing ride.'
> \*'Up from Your Life', *Hourglass*, Columbia, 1997

---

**Activity**

Take each of the words or phrases italicised in the case study in Box 4.2 and frame some questions to explore whether they are gateway phrases into spirituality.

---

One final caveat: once found does not necessarily mean forever held! I have already cited the example of Frankl who struggle to find meaning in the concentration camp.[9] Aleksandr Solzhenitsyn similarly found a sense of meaning, resilience and spirituality sufficient to survive war, Nazi imprisonment and even cancer; a sense of presence from a Higher Power was a feature of his writing.

Perhaps this is one of the factors that differentiate *meaning* from *spirituality*: belief in an exterior Other-based Higher Power spirituality is perhaps more resilient than an inward I-based meaning.

> **Activity: Role models**
>
> Identify three people who have had a positive significance in your life. You many not have known them personally but they do need to have had a major impact. What attitudes, actions, values and/or behaviours did you learn from them and seek to apply in yourself? Did they have one or more 'dark wood' experiences? If so, what did they learn a) while they were still in it; b) looking back at it later?
>
> Identify some people who have had an impact on your spiritual life or beliefs – positively or negatively. Why did they have that impact? What might they say to you in your current situation? Why?
>
> For whom are you – or might you be – a role model? What attitudes, actions, values and/or behaviours would you hope they would take from you?
>
> How might you as a coach use the 'dark wood' metaphor with current clients? What emerging questions might help them begin to explore 'spirituality'?

## Part 4: Rituals

Often one of the most devastating impacts of a crisis is that it deflects us from our routines, the things that give us sense and security through their familiarity. These are often identified as a ritual: a set of actions, performed mainly for their symbolic value. Their primary function is to meet the emotional or spiritual needs of the practitioner and may be of particular value in times of crisis because they give a real sense of familiarity and comfort when all around may seem to be disintegrating. Many organisations have their own rituals. In psychology and therapy the term has a more specialist sense of repetitive actions (such as hand-washing) performed to reduce or relive anxiety or prevent (perceived) bad consequences. Given my earlier cautionary note for coaches dealing with clients in crisis, this is an important distinction that may signpost a boundary being crossed. Nevertheless, because rituals are important due to their symbolic nature they often occur in times of crisis: the widow's daily time spent at her deceased husband's grave; the lucky tie needed for a job interview by someone facing redundancy; the insistence of taking the same unalterable route because on a previous occasion it had avoided an act of terrorism. . .

The importance of rituals undertaken by those in crises lies in what they make 'real'. Of themselves they are innocuous. The crucial thing is what the performer attaches to them. They are a way of making tangible other feelings that are felt more deeply but frequently have not been specifically articulated or even acknowledged by the practitioner. They represent values and beliefs at a much deeper level.[10] And that is precisely why they are so important in coaching.

### Activity

This section poses some questions to help coachees identify rituals that might restore some equilibrium and identify some core values.

1. What are the repetitive, symbolic actions in your family life? (e.g. the holiday rituals). In your working life? Who and what is involved?
2. What values are indicated here?
3. How do the rituals at home and/or work relate to each other? Which would take precedence? What would displace all others?
4. What's missing?

# 5

# Spirituality and business

**Overview**

In Chapter 2 I suggested some definitions of spirituality that included:

> Our innate need to connect the activities of our daily life, our wellsprings of deepest meaning, to something greater than and external to ourselves that compels us beyond ourselves and our narrow self-interests . . . to make a difference.

The previous chapter dealt with coaching in times of crises, when events beyond a person's control have propelled them over the precipice-edge. I argued that the role of coach is to help explore and feel the ensuing darkness and then be a companion for exploring different roads until the relative clarity of new paradigms begins to emerge. I also mentioned the important role of rituals as significant repetitive symbolic actions providing security during this exploration.

While there are clear common threads in these areas and in the writings of the academics and researchers concerning, for example, the positive impact of spirituality on motivation, resilience and sense-making, there are also different interpretations about what exactly it is. Sometimes it is assumed to be *cognitive* (reaching an intellectual understanding about shared values); sometimes *emotional* (about feeling joined or in union); sometimes *behavioural* (these sets of beliefs will result in those sets of actions or behaviours). Most often it is confused with religion, one possible outward expression. In one sense spirituality, rather like beauty, is in the eye of the beholder. Nevertheless it is intrinsically about relationship, connectivity – and a sense of something or someone greater.

In this chapter I consider whether spirituality has any role at all in the workplace, argue that it brings some clear advantages for both the individual and the business itself and then provide a framework for identifying and developing spiritually intelligent leaders.

## Part 1: Is work a suitable context?

If you accept the contention that meaning and spirituality are an intrinsic part of being fully 'human' and given that for many of us in the West work constitutes upwards of one-third of each day for five-sevenths of a week and some 45+ weeks of the year spread over perhaps 50 years, it's difficult to see how it cannot be. We also (rightly or wrongly) often have our identity defined and categorised by 'what (work) do you do?' Exclusion from that sphere can be deeply traumatic. Redundancy or retirement frequently becomes allied with loss of self-identity and purpose.

Work is also the place where, alongside the family context, we are put under the most pressure, see our limitations most stretched and have our weaknesses potentially most exposed. It's the place where significant numbers of people meet their life-partner, whose presence will therefore impact far beyond just the work context. Little wonder then that as the workplace increasingly serves many of the functions previously provided by the community so many workers seem to be seeking at least *meaning* in their workplace and often *spirituality* as well . . .

Is it possible to talk about the spirituality of an organisation? Can organisations manifest spirituality? After all, they only physically exist through their members. There are now decades of research into the culture or cultures of an organisation. Consultants highly skilled in identifying organisations and how to 'change' them have proliferated in recent years, alongside a growing recognition that an organisation's culture is rather more than simply the sum of its parts. Cultural audits of organisations such as charities and, especially, schools suggest that their staff often corporately reflect a standpoint that might be classed as spiritual.

> **Box 5.1**
>
> Some years ago I was part of an inspection of one such school: the Head had written at length before my preliminary visit about the importance they placed on creating an environment that was positive not just for pupils but also staff, parents and governors. She noted with pride the number of visitors who crossed the threshold and commented on the 'atmosphere' that they felt. Although it was explicitly a Church of England school,[1] many of the staff had no faith allegiance and several others came from a faith other than Christianity. But all talked about their commitment to the school's 'spirit' and spoke of seeing their work as a response to values they felt deep within themselves and expressed in their commitment to and hope for the pupils, for other staff and also for other groups across the world. Adults opened doors for pupils; pupils gave way to adults and all appeared to be treated with equal respect, concern and interest. One wall even boasted a display of where teachers had gone for *their* holidays! But what truly made it stand out was the implicit recognition that, while this relatively small school (some 350 pupils) was only a microcosm, it was a microcosm of a greater whole, of which it was an intrinsic and interactive organism (if I may mix metaphors). It was part of something much bigger than itself and hence belonging gave both meaning and impetus.

So the answer to the question that starts this section is, for me, 'yes'. And that puts an additional obligation on those organisations to care for the welfare of their staff. It is in everyone's best interests.

## *Context*

In the past couple of centuries changes in technology, science, tastes, preferences, fashion and society have been myriad. It is now a hundred years since the American FW Taylor introduced the doctrine of scientific management via his seminal book *The Principles of Scientific Management* (1911). Work was increasingly being seen as about process and efficiency. Taylor's central premise was that workers are much like machines and therefore need to be programmed for maximum efficiency; any place for seeking meaning in and from work should therefore be eliminated. In its place arose the assumption that 'work' and 'the rest of life' are completely distinct and non-interchangeable. The previous chapter about crises dealt with some of the unfortunate consequences of that over-simplistic separation.

Unbelievably in this day and age there is still a widespread expectation that employees leave their 'personal' life at the door when they 'clock on', divesting it rather like a soggy raincoat and leaving it to drip unattended. And how often we still hear the end of work referred to as 'the end of the day' as if all that happens afterwards is somehow 'non-time', a half-existence between life (i.e. work) finishing for one day and starting again at clocking-on time the next? Any talk of 'meaning' was, at best, relegated into that shadowy half-life outside work and even then raised the fear of being labelled 'touchy-feely' or 'religious' or downright 'eccentric'. What does this say in terms of Goethe's assertion that the way a person is treated determines what they will become?

But machines we are not.[2] Recent decades have therefore seen a resurgence of the need to find meaning in that area of our life occupying such a significant percentage of our time, effort, commitment and sense of worth. And as that irrepressible search for meaning has re-emerged, there has been increasing evidence from empirical research that there is both an ethical and a commercial benefit in the workforce that, through meaning, finds increased commitment, motivation and output in work.[3] Indeed, recognition of a business' responsibility towards the community of which it is itself a part has both grown and broadened rapidly in recent years. Starting under the banner of Corporate Social Responsibility and a desire to 'give something back' in terms of expertise through voluntary work it has developed into a proactive initiative aligning of good works, good commercial interest and good people-development. Goethe had already understood this.

## Box 5.2

Shortly after the disastrous tsunami of December 2004, an alert executive in global insurer Allianz noticed that they did not receive a single insurance claim. Surely, they reasoned, a disaster on this scale should have had some impact on one of the world's largest insurers? It took little research to prove the obvious answer: the disaster most affected the poorest and most vulnerable, those least likely to afford or access insurance protection. The result? Allianz partnered with charity CARE International, already active with the poorest communities in southern India, to create individually tailored insurance packages for under 8p (11 cents) a day. The villagers designed the products to cover death, medical treatment for injuries in accidents, help with funeral costs and hospital expenses, as well as paying wages during illness. Allianz SE board member Werner Zedelius said: 'Traditionally, poor people cannot afford the premiums for insurance cover, but here we have developed a set of products the community can afford and actually wants to use. For us, micro insurance is a growing social business. We expect it to be profitable within the first year and plan to reinvest any profits into the project to enlarge it further.'[4]

At the beginning of 2009 the US, the UK and many other economies were officially in recession. At the same time, several insolvent banks announced record bonuses, one even having brought them forward to be paid before seeking a government bailout. At the heart of the controversy seemed to be an issue of 'responsibility': a culture of individualisation had grown up that saw no paradox in rewarding individual 'high' performance even though the rest of the organisation was deeply in debt. That there was such a public outcry suggests it was rather more than envy. It seems to represent a deep sense that somehow while this might be legally correct it was morally and ethically wrong, an avoidance of corporate responsibility. Or to use a term from this book, it ignored interconnectivity.

Perhaps at the heart of the different perceptions is that business believes and acts as if the rescue package came from the government and the population believes and acts as if it came from them. 'The bonus figures will be very large and very difficult for the general public to understand' one anonymous insider quoted to *The Times* newspaper, seemingly without irony. 'The debate over bankers' bonuses involves technicalities but is essentially about fairness and justice' wrote a rather more astute insider.[5]

Who defines and judges 'fairness' and 'justice'? There seems to be a mismatch in expectations, with businesses answering or at least tending to assume that they do and the 'general public' feeling they have more than a right to judge. In the past perhaps the dispute would have been referred to the independent arbitration of one of the great institutions: the church for moral issues, the government for legislative and the courts for judicial. But the church has lost its moral imperative, successive governments have tended to become increasingly arms-length in moral, ethical and even legislative guidance and the courts have become immersed in minutiae that to the outsider sometimes appear to be muddying the waters rather than purifying them. In the absence of their touchstone arbitration the issues are thrown back to the individual or small self-inters group. Yet there appears to be a collective consciousness with an intrinsic sense of broadly shared right and wrong.

## *A suitable place for spirituality?*

### Box 5.3

A new police recruit was undergoing weapons training with a cynical old tutor. Very soon he could out-gun not just the other recruits but also the tutor at every juncture. Speed of reflex, accuracy of target-hitting, efficiency of reloading . . . Even when he reached the stage of entering dummy buildings he was instantly able to separate the villainous from the virtuous. Even the cynical tutor had to admit that nothing seemed beyond the recruit's skill.

So in due course he graduated with flying colours and was dispatched to an elite team. Then came the first deployment. All

> went according to the textbook: safe entry, each officer covering another, rooms progressively made safe. Until a door opened. And the young recruit froze. Only the quick-thinking and prompt action of the Unit Commander saved the situation.
>
> Back at the police station the young recruit was mortified. The wise Commanding Officer left him just long enough for arrogance to evaporate and not long enough for despair to take root. Then she called him in. 'You have much skill with the gun and the technique,' she told him, 'But little skill with the mind that fires the gun.'[6]

Many of those we coach have much skill with the technical requirements of their industry and in leadership or we coach them to draw them out. But fewer have the 'skill with the mind' or in this case the skill with the spirit that lets leadership loose to hit the target successfully. I'll return to this later in a section about the characteristics of spiritually intelligent business leaders.

### *Is there an interest?*

According to one recent survey[7] nearly 75 per cent of UK workers would be interested in learning to live the spiritual side of their values at work but 90 per cent of UK managers believe their organisations have not even attempted to discuss the issue of spirituality with their employees. Other surveys have indicated a similar level of interest and titles published in books and journals would also seem to bear this out (see Bibliography).

There seems to be a rising *interest* – but does that mean there is a legitimate *need*? And even if there's a need, is there an added *value*?

### *Is there a need?*

A decade ago, Peter Senge was noting the international rise in interest and articles concerning Spiritual Intelligence, especially amongst leaders. His answer to those who claimed this was 'off-limits' is that it represents a fundamental misunderstanding: 'Spirituality is not about religion. (Rather) it is about the space, freedom and safety to bring our whole being to work.'[8] His research with several hundred business leaders seeking opportunities to explore the area of spirituality and business indicated that 'they wanted people to know they were valued and respected, that they belonged to a community and were not alone, that they could create a culture that let them bring their whole selves to work, not just their hands or their backs or their brains.' Then he adds, tellingly: 'To create such an organization without Spiritual Intelligence would be impossible' (Senge, 2001, p. 552).

Underlying the national debate on the current economic crisis lie two important questions, both in a sense about spirituality:

1. What do we actually want businesses to do?
2. How do we expect them to behave while doing it?

History and experience suggests that in any times of crises, be they financial, political, war or climatic, there is renewed speculation about whether current ways of living, behaving and believing are sustainable. Currently we hear that expressed in terms of whether our current financial models and assumptions are sustainable; what, if anything, will be different once recession lifts and what are the opportunities for realigning priorities. It raises some fundamental questions about existence, survival, sustainability and growth – questions of purpose, meaning and spirituality:

- Does our economic survival and growth depend on constantly increasing profits to shareholders and salaries to workers?
- Is our economy operating in the way we wish for the majority of people, resulting in sustainable and equitable creation and distribution of wealth?
- What do we want our economy to do – and why?
- What is 'the market rate' and do governments have the right to interfere? Do they have the right *not* to?
- Is that incompatible with equality and support for the least-privileged in our societies?
- Are our businesses a microcosm of our economy? Do they formulate the economy – or does the economy formulate them?

SPIRITUALITY AND BUSINESS   109

- What difference would it make if we were to replace 'economy' with 'society' or 'community'?
- What are acceptable standards of behaviour – and what are not? Who decides?
- Who monitors, how and why? Is the sole arbiter compliance with the law (governance) or is there an ethical dimension? If so, what part should it play?
- Is it incompatible with inexorable growth?
- And does it give each of us the intrinsic sense of satisfaction, enjoyment and contentment that we seek?
- What are the principles, the pillars on which we would want all of these based?

It seems to me there are two specific and distinct needs here. One is the need expressed by workers within an organisation to be able to bring their whole self to work in order to be more fully who they are; the other is the need for clear leadership in those organisations, and I'll return to this in a later section below. Absolutely there is a need.

## *Is there a value?*

First, some recent quotes:

> Organisations whose mission or superordinate goals make a difference in the wider community, are consistent with personal values, and which reflect these values in their policies, inspire greater levels of employee commitment, motivation, performance, innovation and loyalty than their competitors.
>
> (Poole, 2006)

> Spirituality positively affects employee and organisational performance by enhancing intuitive abilities and individual capacity for innovation, as well an increasing personal growth, employee commitment and responsibility.
>
> (Neck and Milliman, 1994, p. 9)

> I do believe strongly in leading in a spiritual way. It keeps you from doing many short-term tactical actions

that are often wrong for the business and the people. It also gives you immense courage to stand tall against politics.

(Janiece Webb, Motorola, 2004)[9]

And more specifically:

you have to take the whole individual into account. The workaholic is to be avoided because their drive does not generally inspire a team. It can actually be abusive. Those who are spiritual and make room for other things – family, charity, reflection, even prayer – and are able to put things into context make the more inspiring leaders.

(Robinson, 2008)

In Chapter 2 I used Thompson's definition of spirituality: 'the way in which people connect the activities of their daily life with their wellsprings of deepest meaning.' Most organisations want their staff to feel part of that organisation rather than operate in isolation. Questions of spirit arise as soon as we ask about connectivity and meaning. This is no different in the workplace to anywhere else. If individual employees within an organisation embrace that connectivity and a spiritual perspective it impacts both their internal motivation and their external actions. But can the same be said about an organisation? Is there such a thing as organisational spirituality? There is no doubt that organisations have a culture that is distinct from the individuals who work there: it may be consistent with their values or it may be subtly different and occasionally in direct contrast. More accurately, it reflects the behaviours of the leaders throughout the organisation: what they implicitly and explicitly reward or punish, commend or criticise. Thus it is perfectly possible to create an organisational culture that permits, supports or encourages a spiritual dimension. And research suggests[10] that such an atmosphere is likely to improve business performance because:

- Staff who find meaning in their work are more motivated and produce better-quality work.

- Retention rates are boosted.
- This becomes a magnet for new staff.

What a shame we so often settle for an uncomfortable tension between our own sense of purpose and the constraining demands of our organisation – to the detriment of both.

*Economic value*

Do the debates in the financial sector in 2008 and beyond really offer insights into the *economic value* of embedding spirituality in the DNA of the workplace? An economic imperative rather than a 'nice-to-have'?

The gateway that seems most apposite is that of performance bonuses. What has been of significance in the very public discussions is not the ethicality of bonuses *per se* but the premise on which they are awarded: between individual reward versus corporate accountability, between 'I deserve to be well-rewarded because I have performed well' versus 'I am a part of something bigger, to which my efforts in part are contributed'. The awareness of the part played by the individual in the interconnected webs of relation to those around them is the core of SQ. It is through the reactions of those around us, in community we most often become aware of a hitherto-unrecognised deficiency in outlook or behaviour as we develop as people. In the case of performance bonuses, especially in the financial sector, the reaction of members of the wider society indicates a deep nerve has been touched: 'This just doesn't feel to be right'. The reactions of the wider community of connectivity can be a good early warning that something is wrong at the individual level; SQ can be an effective antidote to excessive egocentricity.[11]

In recent years analysts such as Gareth Morgan (1997) have broadened the language and understanding of the symbols we use to think about organisations and our interplay with them beyond the solely mechanistic. The power of symbols is widely recognised and symbolism sits at the heart of spirituality. Whereas a few years ago the onus might have been on proving that spirituality had any part whatsoever to play in the workplace never mind any value to add, nowadays the onus might well be what right does the coach have *not* to raise it. Witness:

- the higher priority given by graduates and those under 25 to working for organisations that have an unequivocal commitment to corporate responsibility, ethical policies and personal development,
- the growing recognition that ethically based policies have not only a social but also a trading competitive edge (and the growing significance of Islamic banking practices),
- the rise in fair-trade markets,
- the burgeoning of SMEs[12] with a social-transformation focus,
- the accusations of use of child-labour by subsidiaries of Nike and other multi-nationals that led to product boycotts, forcing businesses to change their practices and monitor more closely,

and many more . . .

Of course these are not of themselves necessarily issues of meaning nor of spirituality nor indeed of any awareness of wider external obligation; they are laudable aims in themselves. But they do suggest that a growing number of people have concerns and interests and commitments that willingly recognise the interplay of personal behaviour, business values, community, and society on a global impact. Indeed, one of the most damning criticisms of British bankers made by the British City Minister Lord Myners was that 'they had no sense of the broader society around them.'[13] And recent product- or company-boycotts demonstrate that it can be only a small step from criticism to commercial blockade.

If business leaders *are* to recognise that the wider society does expect businesses to play their part in the 'broader society around them' and if that is to be anything more than a perfunctory dabbling in a corporate social responsibility model little more than the occasional donation to a community raffle, they will need help. Indeed if they are to recognise and truly embrace the paradigm shift advocated as the best option for a sustainable economic future they will need *lots* of help. For the questions they need to ask go to the very heart of what we want our business and society to achieve both locally and globally. They challenge some deeply held assumptions. Our current iteration of Western trading may have reached its mid-life crisis and may need an injection of compassion if it is to survive at all. There are issues of identity, place, purpose, consequence and connectivity.

*The value of interconnectivity*

More positively, these financial crises have cemented recognition of a global interconnectedness. If the connectivity image of the butterfly wing in the Amazon sparking a tornado in Japan had become the source of some humour, the impact of a defaulting mortgagee in rural Mississippi on the ordinary resident in Manchester has been all too sobering; the failure of Northern Rock Building Society in the UK in 2007/8 heralded a tsunami that washed over large swathes of the world. And the solutions applied to these problems have impacts no less global: subsidies to one industry to avoid mass redundancies can give false price-protection that bankrupts other companies in another part of the world. A drop in sales of cell phones in the US can lead to redundancies in outsourced call support centres in India and factory closures in China. Simplistic and metaphorical, but the message of global interconnectedness is clear.

They are interconnected and the common theme is a search for meaning, impact, purpose and potential, a recognition that we need to move beyond the West's individualistic and self-centred outlook to a global linkage, a sense of care for others as well as for ourselves and a recognition that each has a part to play in a broader purpose.

Some argue that this alternative approach would sound the death-knell to stakeholder investment and our standard of living, or dismiss it as mere fluffy New Age mumbo-jumbo. But there are sufficient examples of leaders who *do* manage this tricky combination and add extraordinary value to prevent us dismissing it too readily. With a moment's reflection, there is no shortage of successful people who demonstrate the centrality of spiritual awareness, a search for meaning, in their lives: Desmond Tutu, Bill Clinton . . . We'll return to what these characteristics might be later in the chapter. For the moment, suffice to say that each stresses the importance of recognising our interconnectivity.

> **Box 5.4 Graham Williams: Reading the signs**
>
> Over the past 30 years Graham has started and turned around numerous rapid growth companies. He has taken four companies from start-up to approximately $100m turnover plus turned around successfully other companies via mergers and acquisitions. His work has spanned the continents; his businesses have spanned the sectors. He is by any measure a very successful business leader. 'For me, it was just success, achievement and then moving on to the next success.'
>
> Yet Graham would say it is only in the past couple of years he's begun to understand the central place of spirituality and to consciously put it into his business dealings. So has there been a dramatic change in the way he operates? 'No. I realised that for me to feel successful, I need to have four things: razor-sharp vision, desire and passion, a natural ability, and to want to help people'. In some ways, this reflects the growth from *meaning* to *spirituality*, from EQ to SQ. 'At one stage we won 36 out of 38 decision evaluations – and I focused on the two and not the 36! It's getting back to – and sticking to – my basic principles. I had a very successful country managing director who crossed the line in terms of values and principle. It was tempting to bend the rules but I fired him, recognising that it could have made me less successful. In fact, the other offices saw that as a great example of principle and performed better.' It was about strategic overview and awareness of impact of authenticity, the greater good. It also had a positive economic outcome.
>
> So what's been the result of this resurgent recognition of the place of spirituality in his life and his business? 'I am different – not in my behaviours or principles towards others. I've always treated people with respect, been transparent in my dealings, tried to behave to high ethical standards. The change has been in me. By letting go, removing ego and arrogance, I can still be successful, have lots of money, huge desire and have harmony inside. It's not been a loss but a gain.'

Nowadays I come across very few leaders who would say that a quest for meaning or spirituality is a *negative* force; at worst, it might be considered an irrelevance. Most seem to recognise, both in themselves and others, that finding a sense of meaning and connection, an awareness of something or someone greater than oneself, does indeed add value. So why is it not universally accepted?

## Part 2: Overcoming barriers

*Organisationally* there seems to be an instinctive fear partly of the unfamiliar, the 'not done that before' and partly of the overshadowing misinterpretation of equal opportunities and faith. And as 'faith' has increasingly been viewed as an individual rather than a corporate activity, so it has slipped into being an issue about protecting individuals' 'rights'. Perhaps proactively replacing the word 'faith' with 'spirituality' would not only widen its application but also allow it to sit more comfortably at the heart (the soul) of the organisation.

> **Box 5.5 WorldBlu**
>
> *WorldBlu* is a commercial organisation working in leadership development and human capital. Founder Traci Fenton provides an illustration of the place of spirituality in both its foundation and its operation: 'Sitting on the beach, pondering the essence of *WorldBlu*'s work, I was struck by the brilliance of the blue around me. The sky and ocean were enormous. There was something in all that blue that made me feel like anything was possible. I felt, at that moment, a dramatic sense of limitlessness and freedom. If freedom was a color, I reasoned, it must be blue. Our name captures our desire to design "blu" environments within companies all over the world, rooted in the principles of freedom, democracy, and possibility.'

For the *coachee* this may raise deeply uncomfortable issues: the fear of what others might think or challenges around the ethicality of the business in which they are engaged (the tobacco industry, for example), or the behaviours of certain parts of the business (e.g. exploitation of workers in other countries) or the practices expected of employees (e.g. dubious selling techniques). And even if they are in organisations deeply committed to open discussion and acceptance of diversity, the informal 'coffee-cup' conversations may in practice subtly undermine or not so subtly ridicule any mention of faith, beliefs, worship, religion or spirituality. The fear may only be in the mind of the coachee, but their perception is their reality. It is a barrier rather than a gateway. Even if there's willingness, finding a terminology can be problematic. There seems to be a paucity of neutral vocabulary with shared meaning. Little wonder complete avoidance is viewed as preferable to the risk and implications of potentially causing offence.

The *coach* may well echo 'all of the above – and more!' To raise anything to do with spirituality may feel like a risk of loss of reputation or professional credibility; fear of being perceived as intruding on the personal rather than the professional, feeling we have neither the skill nor the experience, even our own preferences all play a part. It may also raise ethical questions for the coach. After all, what I'm suggesting means the coach taking coachees into an arena that may not have previously occurred to them and which they have not themselves raised, thus posing questions about the coach's right to do this leading and whether they might be accused of undue influencing.

We do need to be aware and beware this. But I would argue that effective, professional coaching often involves raising new thoughts with coachees and organisations, of challenging some preconceptions. That is part of our duty. It only becomes wrong if our motivation is to impose our own view rather than help the development of the coachee or if we seek to doggedly pursue it in the face of persistent reluctance on behalf of the coachee. The prize on offer, if it can be won, is a greater integration at the heart (or rather soul) of our coachees with accruing benefits to them, their organisations and those nearest to them.

## *The value proposition*

So there is a rising tide of debate about what we want our businesses to do and to be in our societies; there are increasing numbers of organisations at least experimenting with putting spiritual ideas in place; and there is increasing evidence that tackling issues of meaning and spirituality serves the best interests of employees *and* adds to business bottom line efficiency and profitability.

How might this be done? Various research studies[14] have concluded that organisations able to inspire employee loyalty to a higher 'cause' substantially outperform their peers because of increased motivation and commitment. Increasingly evidence suggests that those organisations undertaking a similar commitment to and with their customers engender greater customer loyalty in times of downturn or mistakes and increased peer-recommendation and loyalty. The UK's Co-Operative Banking Group, for instance, has for more than 15 years claimed not to invest in or fund various businesses such as the fur or armaments industries because its members have specifically raised ethical objections and guided them to principles embracing care for others, community responsibility and sustainability. Not only has it survived recent banking traumas relatively unscathed, it has seen both its scale of investors and its business expenditure grow.

Let's return to the story of David and OMG International – but with a caveat! Although this is based on a real-life story, it is very unusual and I've included it not because it's representative but because it shows what's possible with some effective coaching. Not every opportunity will go like this.

## *Case study: David – Part two*

In Chapter 2, David was wrestling with what 'wanting the best for his family' might mean, not just under his own definition but also that of his wife and of his children. He began to recognise that both he and his wife had a different expectation of what constituted the balance between work and life and to understand that he might find part of his fulfilment outside work – even as a male struggling with the self-imposed expectation of being bread-winner and provider. While recognising that for some people this may well entail a major career-change into voluntary or not-for-profit work, or indeed into early retirement, David has recognised that for him his drive and passion is still for his work with OMG. He has negotiated some boundaries with his wife but been assured that she supports his need to be successful at work and that this will need flexible working hours as long as there's also some positive payback. In essence his is a search for fulfilment and meaning. As I said in Chapter 2, 'meaning is what we draw from our experiences, the way in which we organise them and explain them in order to make sense of them'; I compared it to the formation of a jewel and the need to recognise its value. In this section of the coaching, David and his coach are working on creating the sense-making of meaning for him.

The agreed purpose of this next coaching session is to explore what that might actually look like when expressed in his business context. We join the session after the formalities have been exchanged, the goals identified and there has been a résumé of the previous sessions . . .

Coach: Now, you've said what you'd like to cover in this session, a clearer idea of your next steps over the next few years, so let's take a few minutes reviewing what options there might be and the extent to which each of these might make of each of your strengths and needs. And as we've agreed, I'll prompt you particularly around questions of what will give you the best sense of satisfaction, of achievement . . . so, as part of your preparation, David, I asked you to think of three occasions in the last few years where you've felt really proud of something you've achieved . . .

*Example 1*

David: My sister Zoe works for The Gang. They work with kids who've missed out on school or left early or can't get jobs. About five years ago they'd been planning to launch an initiative to celebrate what young people could achieve, to challenge some of the adverse publicity about young people. She'd got the basic idea of what she wanted but she needed a good title for it and some idea of how to get it noticed, so she asked me to get involved. I'd got a couple of weeks' holiday owing so I met some of the young people she wanted to highlight. Her idea was to ask each of their regions to bring a few people to London and get someone to interview them and then announce a winner. But once I'd met a few of them I realised there were just so many suitable candidates doing such great things and often really against the odds. It really inspired me; in fact it still makes the hairs on my neck stand up even now just talking about it. I really felt there was a sense of purpose about it. So I suggested she had some regional heats because that would allow more to be involved and it would create local media interest as well. Somehow the title of High Fives just came out and stuck. They've got five regions so each region had five finalists and the top one became one of the High Fives sent to the final. We persuaded a couple of rap stars to host the event and it was really successful. In fact, we even managed to get sponsorship so they made money as well!

## *Example 2*

David: In my second job, when I started no one seemed to quite know why I was there or what I was supposed to be doing! The boss had appointed me but then had been taken ill and was off for about three months. Anyway, it was such a horrible experience for me and so wasteful for the company that when the CEO got back I told him so. And to his credit he listened and then said, 'Sounds like you've got yourself a job then!' Teach me to open my big mouth! He redrafted my job description so that I had time to do it. There were about 200 people working on the site so I asked 20 of them what they thought newcomers should be told and then for a year I asked everyone who joined, both when they joined and after six and nine months. From that I devised a programme where they spent a couple of days in each department and then shadowed one of the board members for three days. They also got a mentor and various other things as well. Anyway, the upshot was that retention improved and I won a Regional Business Development Award! I was really pleased because it meant no one else had to go through the uncertainty that I'd been through. And I was proud that people in my profession also recognised it. It's the only award I've ever won and it still sits on my shelves at home. In fact sometimes when I've had a really bad day, I'll notice it and I can almost hear the applause ringing in my ears again.

*Example 3*

David: My third story comes from when I'd just left school. I took a gap year before going to university and spent three months in Malawi teaching English in a school. I was young and idealistic, I think I felt I was on a mission to change the world! It was really strange at first because I wasn't much older than a lot of the kids; I'd only just finished school myself and I was hardly a trained teacher. But they didn't mind, they were just so keen to learn. Some of them walked for two hours each day just to get there. And somehow their parents had to find the money to pay for their schooling. There were hardly any books or any other resources. And they were so happy, just squealing and laughing all the time. One day about halfway though my time I was sitting under a tree taking a break; it was hot, the kids had been in a stuffy room for three hours and yet they'd worked so hard. And they were still smiling. And suddenly I realised just how much about my school I'd just taken for granted. Actually not just taken for granted but also complained about: boring lessons, having to do homework, getting up early . . . It was a real shock, I felt so ashamed. In fact

for a few days I even decided I'd chuck the idea of uni and stay where I was, helping out and at least feeling I was making some difference, some positive contribution. Those kids and their parents seemed to have something that we'd lost. I still don't know what it was. At first I thought it was a goal, a drive to get a good education so they'd get a good job and earn some decent money. And that was certainly part of it. But there was something more, something deeper about them. The closest I got was when I came back and someone said to me, 'That's the problem with the West – we know the cost of everything and the value of nothing'. They understood value, they had a sense of meaning in life that I didn't. Of course, by the end of the three months I was tired, excited about seeing my family again and just seemed to roll on into uni and then into work. But I sometimes wonder: what if I had stayed there, how might my life have been different?
(There's a long silence.)

### Activity

1. Spend a few minutes reflecting on David's examples. What are the common themes between them? What strikes you about them? What might you ask him next in the context of spirituality – the gateway terms and phrases?
2. David uses some gateway words and phrases that point to something deeper going on. Re-read his examples, making a note of them.

And back to the case study . . .

In effect, this section begins to crystallise the jewel of 'meaning' for David.

Coach: From these stories, what would you say makes you come alive?

David: Well – as I thought about them it struck me there's something about making a difference to people, about doing something new, that challenges and innovates. I started to look at all sorts of things and just ask the question, 'Does it really matter, in the broader scope of things?' I wrote down that having my achievements recognised by others is probably important to me as well. I'm sure it shouldn't be, but it is. Talking about it now I guess it's about finding a sense of purpose, a sense of meaning. Actually, it's 'what am I called to do?'

Coach: From the stories you've just told me, what are the significant words or phrases that stand out in your mind?

David: Good question . . . I think I said in Malawi, 'I felt I was making a difference, some positive contribution'. That's the story that still feels like unfinished business. I think it's because at the time, when I was actually there, the people seemed so serene and content despite their circumstances. In fact that seemed to make me even more angry about the poverty and disease they suffered. But then I turned my back on them, I just dropped back into the busy life, the expectations as soon as I got home. I suppose it's made me think again about how they could find so much in having so little. And I seem to have so much and yet feel I've got so little – of real value.

Coach: You mentioned 'unfinished business'. What's 'unfinished'?

David: Two dimensions, I think, and I'm not quite sure which comes first. One is that I still feel I've got lots of things I could contribute to make a difference. The other is my need to feel fulfilled, that somehow there's a purpose to all this.

Coach: So – it sounds as if your key things are around making a difference, innovation and recognition? And meaning?

(David nods.)

What might give you 'a sense of meaning'?

David: Well, that's where I get stuck. It's tempting to think that if I volunteered back in Malawi for six months it would solve both of them. But I don't think it would.

|        | I'd be working on my symptoms, not my disease, or rather my dis-ease! I need to work out *why* I need to do this first. And there's still my family to think of and all the other practical details. |
|--------|---|
| Coach: | Yes, that's clearly important to you and something we can come back to later on. But is there anything else that strikes you about your example stories? |
| David: | ...Yes, actually. I seem to work best and feel more fulfilled when there's a challenge, especially if the challenge can improve things for other people. |
| Coach: | Anything else? |
| David: | No, I don't think so. Why? |
| Coach: | I was struck by the points at which your body language changed, when you looked and sounded much more animated. And there were two particular phrases where I noticed it, when you said: 'There was a sense of purpose about it', and then, 'How might my life have been different?' It seems to me both of these are about what you've also mentioned, looking for a sense of meaning. So what are the things that give you a sense of meaning? |
| David: | Well, I guess we've already mentioned *challenge*, which is about bringing out the full *potential* in me and in others. Then something about *purpose*, about making a difference, making life better for others. But I think there's something more, there's something external, about feeling *drawn*, almost like a magnet, to other people with whom I feel a real connection. I suppose there's stuff about what I want to *do* and stuff about what I want to *be*. But there's also something about what you once called sense-making, about finding meaning... |
| Coach: | OK. Earlier, you said this is about, 'What am I called to do?' That's the point where I think we should start next time. And, yes, I know we haven't finished today yet... |

> **Activity**
>
> The activity at the end of this chapter (Table 5.1) lists some of my suggestions about David's gateway words and phrases and also gives an opportunity for you to practise. I'd like to suggest you do that now before returning to David and the rest of this chapter . . .

Coach: What might you do next to help you find meaning?

David: Well, I guess it could be a good moment to think about voluntary work again!

Coach: What would you gain from that?

David: I'd certainly get the challenge. And it would give me a sense of purpose. In fact, as I think about it, it does seem to tick most if not all the boxes . . . The trouble is, the more I think about it, the more, deep down, it somehow doesn't feel the right thing.

Coach: So you appear to be saying you *think* it's ticking the boxes but you *feel* it's the wrong route? Your head agrees, your heart doesn't? What might you lose?

David: My job, possibly. I don't think OMG would be very happy about me going off for six months! And actually I think I'd miss quite a few of the people I work with. I think I'd miss some of the intellectual stimulation that I get from my work. And of course I'd miss my wife: but I think I could explain it to her and she'd probably agree.

Coach: OK – that's what you think. Now what about what you feel?

David: I feel it wouldn't give me what I'm looking for. And actually, although I think my wife would agree intellectually – she'd see the logic – I feel it would put a real strain on our relationship. And my kids would hate it.

Coach: What other options can you think of?

David: Well, I guess I might start some voluntary work here, maybe go back to The Gang with Zoe. That would certainly be challenging. And would make a difference. But it's just like the Malawi idea: intellectually, it make sense, it ticks all the boxes. But emotionally, it just doesn't feel right. The trouble is, I'm not used to thinking emotionally.

Coach: Isn't that the point? You can't think emotionally and you can't feel intellectually. They're completely different things. Both are important, but both tell us different things. And it's important to consider what both are saying.
(David nods.)
Any other options?

David: Stay where I am!

Coach: What would have to happen for you to feel fulfilled by doing that?

David: Well, I guess if the company could find me something challenging that gave me a sense of meaning and that made a real difference. Though I've no idea what that might be!

Coach: What might you do to find out?

David: Actually, that's a really good point. I've got a meeting with the CEO scheduled for next week. I could ask him what he thinks.

Coach: Suppose you took a proposal to him. What might that look like?

David: I guess it's what I just said, a project that gives me a sense of meaning and that makes a real difference. Something that gives me challenge and the chance for recognition but puts something back into society ... Actually, I feel quite excited about that – if I can just find the way of doing it. It makes sense and ... (He pauses and grins.) It feels right too! I'll give it some thought between now and then.

A week later, the following email arrives in the coach's inbox:

Well, quick update! Went into the CEO's office all lined up with my arguments and thoughts to convince him why he should let me do this and I didn't get beyond my first few words about meaning and making a difference before he jolted back in his seat in surprise. Turns out he'd been thinking about a new project idea but couldn't think how to get it off the ground and who might lead it. Anyway, cutting a long discussion short – we've agreed that in two months time, I'll be given two days a week to recruit and head up a team to develop a new and affordable malaria drug for the developing world. I get a challenge, a chance to make my mark again in all the things that I'm best at. We get to make a difference and I can stay in the commercial sector.

### *Case study: David – Part three*

It's six months later when the next session takes place. David has been out to Botswana with OMG's partner video production company to advertise the project to the rest of the company and begin to draw a team together. Once again, the pleasantries have been exchanged and the session has been running for about 20 minutes.

David: . . . Funnily enough, what really made things start to click into place was working with the film crew. I'd done a lot of the business plan before I even went out there. But in the pre-visit discussions they'd asked me to think and speak as graphically as possible so that it came over better on the screen. And that made all the difference. Somehow it made me look beyond the surface, to look for the story behind what was happening. So instead of just filming the first few key workers in our building we filmed them at home as well to give people back here a flavour of what life was like in Gaborone and in the surrounding villages. We told their stories, what they were hoping to get from working for us and what they brought to us. They mostly talked about the difference that the drug would make for malaria sufferers and we filmed some of the doctors in the clinics near to the border with Zimbabwe where they'd had a recent outbreak of malaria. What struck me was their sense of belonging, of being part of something wider. It wasn't defeatism, a cop-out from reality. They really felt they were an interconnected part. In fact, I rather made a fool of myself. I was talking to one of the village elders in Bobirwa and he made some comment about being glad he wasn't part of the financial upheavals in the West. I couldn't believe he knew about that in this remote Eastern region of Botswana and it must have showed on my face: he just laughed and said, 'We do have the internet, you know!' But then he said something that really set me thinking: 'Sometimes it takes those outside the myth to challenge the blindness of those inside it.'

Coach: What did you feel he meant by that? What lies outside the myth?

David: I felt that his point was we'd become so weighed down with our technologies and sophistication that we'd lost connectivity to the simpler but more profound, what he called 'the spirit of the soul'. That's what I noticed about so many of the people, they had this spiritual awareness that gave them a sense of belonging, meaning and purpose, a place in something much larger outside themselves but of which they were an essential part. And because of that they were somehow better able to cope. Of course when I said this back at work, the cynics said it was just a way of them making excuses for why their life was so unfair and demeaning. But if they'd looked into their eyes they'd have understood: somehow these people were more complete than most people I've ever met. It was an amazing attachment to their country but to something much more than that as well. They already saw me as part of that interconnectivity. Just think what a difference it would make if we could harness that serenity and motivation for OMG back here!

Coach: Can you draw out just a few specific words (verbs not adjectives) that made the difference and you'd want to import?

David: (He reruns mental pictures from his trip.) 'Compassionate'; 'Wise'; 'Accepting'; 'Calm/centred'; 'Passionate, committed and excited about opportunities'; 'Authentic'... But actually, behind all of that they had a real feeling of being part of something much bigger, almost like a magnet attracting us and drawing us out, something sacred, spiritual – whatever that means. Actually, the phrase that really hit me like a bolt of lightening was the Bobirwa Elder who talked about the Spirit of the Soul. That really attracted me.

---

**Activity**

What particular skills does David's coach use that enable David to move into the realm of meaning and of spirituality?

Proactively seek out occasions when your coachees are using words about values and/or meaning and encourage them to explore these more deeply, including how they might be expressed in action. (Note that for some, finding meaning at work may entail them operating in a more development-centred style of leadership, or perhaps becoming a mentor; it might be as a union representative or a school governor or on the board of a charity or community group.)

Use *either* the case study with David *or* a past coaching client of your own for this activity. Depending on your preferred learning style, you might write the story or the script of the remainder of the coaching session. Another approach would be to work with a well-briefed colleague who takes David's part, allowing you to draw on both your prepared questions and those that arise as the scenario unfolds. Equally you might discuss the details so far with a colleague and then discuss how it might unfold, exploring different routes and their implications. Remember that on this occasion it's about trying to explore meaning and spirituality, so don't get sidetracked!

---

## Part 3: The characteristics of spiritually intelligent business leaders

In previous chapters I've argued that the past few decades have seen a significant broadening in our understanding of the complexity of 'intelligence'. Some writers now claim there are as many as eight multiple intelligences. Daniel

Goleman developed probably the most famous and widespread: Emotional Intelligence (EQ). More recently EQ has been linked with Spiritual Intelligence (SQ). In many ways, SQ has been a development from the ability to process knowledge and understanding of *facts and data* (IQ) to the ability to process *feelings and emotions* of our fellow humans (EQ); from that EQ has then been developed to the ability to process that which gives *meaning and purpose* to our lives and, crucially, the lives of others (SQ). Each involves skills; SQ particularly involves envisioning, inspiration, and a search for a transcendent meaning of benefit both to ourselves and to others.

The American researcher into spirituality and business, Cindy Wigglesworth, poses two key questions in her workshops with business leaders that are useful gateway questions for coaches as well:

1. Who are the spiritual leaders that you have admired in your life – living, dead, real or fictional, unknown or family?
2. What are the character traits that cause you to admire them?

The typical responses that she encountered (loving, kind, forgiving, peaceful, courageous, honest, generous, persistent, faithful, wise, inspirational) include words that are clearly spiritual and indicate some key characteristics that define the spiritually aware leader and that they use to bring added value to their organisation and its people.

Many authors and even more books and articles outline the features of successful leaders; here I have concentrated only on those that might be deemed 'spiritual'.

### Activity

What do you think it might look and feel like to work for spiritually intelligent business leaders? What sets them apart? What would their organisations/departments look and feel like?

So what are those characteristics and what exactly sets them apart? I think they come under four main groupings.

## *Time and space*

One of the characteristics of leaders with a highly developed SQ seems to be a different perception of 'time': not that they have more or less of it but that they have a particular way of spending it. Typically they will spend more time in focused reflection, stillness and being. Indeed, research by Californian Professor Andre Delbecq[15] suggests they deliberately 'enter the workplace mindfully', frequently pausing in the car or before an important meeting or decision to 'reflect on their calling as a leader'. Delbecq says his research indicates that as well as a heightened awareness of 'time' they also have a heightened sense of 'space', often shifting their gaze slightly to take in a favourite icon or symbol, a painting or even visiting a quiet space such as a fountain in order to create 'in-between' moments and thus arrive more focused and empowered. Korac-Kakabadse[16] argues that a core competence is contemplation since this is what enables people to extract wisdom from experience.

## *Tolerance of imperfection*

This is not the same as acceptance of second-best. It is a recognition that none are perfect, that few come to work intending to do a bad job, but that nothing less than a striving for excellence in self and others can fulfil potential. It also recognises that mistakes often stimulate the most effective learning.

## *Servant leadership*

This is perhaps too easily dismissed as a recipe for avoiding taking responsibility, as doormat rather than doorkeeper. But as Greenleaf describes it,[17] leaders who desire to serve others will be seeking a response to these questions:

- Will my influence enable all the people to grow and develop as people?

- Will those people being served become healthier, wiser, freer, more likely themselves to become servant leaders?
- What will be the effect on the least privileged in society?

In other words, they have a gardening role as cultivators of rounded human beings. The CEO of one multinational fast-food chain reputedly used to send newly appointed managers a set of Russian dolls; inside the smallest was a handwritten note reminding them that if they only appointed people less able than themselves, they would soon cease to exist; if they appointed those more able, then the sky's the limit.

## *Radiators of peace*

They have their own inner sense of peace, equanimity and meaning, of their place in the grand order of things and their mission to make things different and better for others in response to what they themselves have received. This is obvious to those around them and is generally independent of immediate circumstances. They remain in equilibrium even under pressure or crisis. Their behaviours remain consistent and their vision and passion remain focused.

Other characteristics might include abundance, authenticity, compassion, discernment, forgiveness, freedom, honesty, gratitude, healing, humility, integrity, interconnectedness, meaning-making, mission, nurturing, peace, sense-making, service, stature, stillness, transformation, trust, vision, wisdom.

## *Measuring their skill*

Given that SQ developed out of the study of EQ and ways of measuring it, it is hardly surprising that similar research has taken place into how to identify and 'measure' SQ. Wigglesworth, for example,[18] has proposed that the specific qualities or characteristics of spiritually intelligent leaders contain quadrants similar to those put forward by Goleman and Boyatzis,[19] arguing that the stages are both developmental and progressive so that it is necessary to achieve some familiarity with one quadrant in order to move into

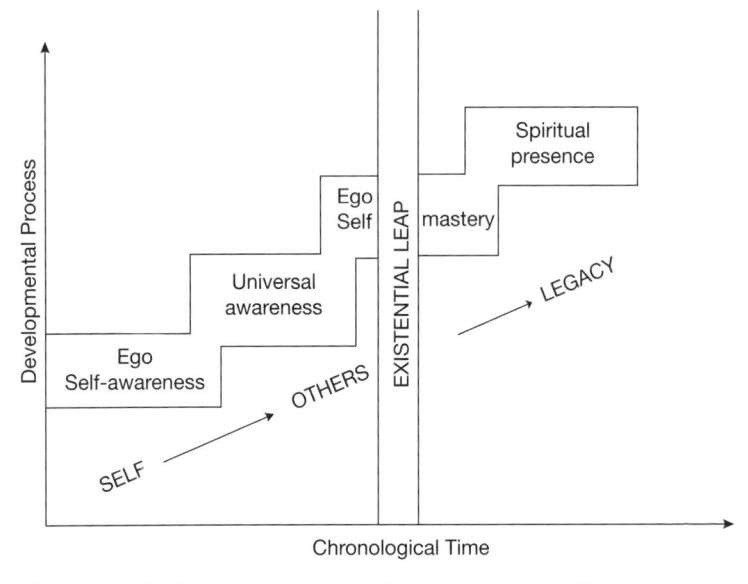

*Figure 5.1* **The four quadrants and development over time**

the next; they are ascending a spiral. Figure 5.1 shows how Wigglesworth's quadrants might fit on the Model last refined in Chapter 3. It also shows them to be both developmental and yet overlapping. Once again The Existential Leap provides the chasm and not all will cross.

Wigglesworth argues that these quadrants encompass 21 measurable behaviours:

- Ego self / Higher Self-Awareness
    1. Awareness of own worldview
    2. Awareness of life purpose (mission)
    3. Awareness of values hierarchy
    4. Complexity of inner thought
    5. Awareness of Ego self/Higher Self

- Universal Awareness
    6. Awareness of interconnectiveness of all life
    7. Awareness of worldview of others
    8. Breadth of time/space perception
    9. Awareness of limitations/power of human perception

10. Awareness of spiritual laws
  11. Experience of transcendent oneness
- Ego self / Higher Self Mastery
  12. Commitment to spiritual growth
  13. Keeping Higher Self in charge
  14. Living your purpose and values
  15. Sustaining your faith/spirituality
  16. Seeking guidance from Spirit
- Social Mastery and Spiritual Presence
  17. Being a wise and effective spiritual teacher/mentor
  18. Being a wise and effective change agent
  19. Taking compassionate and wise decisions
  20. Being a calming, healing presence
  21. Being aligned with the ebb and flow of life

Any of these might be present in any type of leader; it is their combination and their context that produce the *spiritually aware* leader. This spiritually aware leader is also not afraid to deliver the hard messages and to 'wash feet as well as apply the whip'.[20] When coaching in this area our work is to help our clients explore what it means to develop these 21 skills and deploy them collectively to make a difference.

Since the appropriate leadership style is selected on the basis of 'with these people, at this time, in these circumstances', it is perfectly possible to be an SQ-aware leader while employing (most of) the existing recognised leadership styles since it is about the state of 'being' from which the actions then flow: leading from the inside out.

## Part 4: Further activities

### *Activity 1*

Who do you admire – alive or dead, fictional or real – as a spiritual leader? What traits or characteristics cause you admire in them?

Typically this might include honesty, integrity, authenticity, compassionate, wise, humble, committed to helping others, etc. They move people emotionally, physically and mentally, while at the same time actively role-modelling; they *pull* but not towards themselves so much as to the something greater out there. That is to say, they are emotionally aware, have a strategic overview awareness of the impact of their attitudes and actions on those around them in the organisation but also in the community and an interconnectedness that might ultimately be global. Moreover they seek the highest ethical standards and the greatest good for the greatest number. They are likely to describe or consider this as their mission, their contribution or their payback to the world. Small wonder that leaders who possess these characteristics, habits and behaviours make a success of what they do: most organisations would pay a premium to employ people like them. Put another way, the characteristics that define and set apart leaders who have a high SQ are those highly sought after by organisations. It's unfortunate that organisations don't more actively encourage the culture of spirituality that would grow them.

## *Activity 2*

This activity could be used with coachees to help them *reconnect passion and dreams with work and beyond* . . . or simply use it to see what it reveals.

### *Step 1: Learning from the past*

- Draw a lifeline, from childhood onwards. Above the line mark the positive events; lows below. Markers might include values such as most fulfilled; most excited; most deflated; etc.
- If there were sudden changes, what triggered them?
- Are there underlying themes?
- Where was your vision at its strongest?
- When were your values most obvious?
- When did you feel most fulfilled? That you had most meaning?

*Step 2: Surveying the present*

- Where is the current life-point?
- Are you currently living your values? In what way(s)?
- Have your dreams changed over this timeline period?
- Are you having fun?

*Step 3: Identifying core values*

- What are the areas of your life that are important to you? (E.g. family, friends, work, sport, spirituality, fitness).
- What are your core values, those that anchor your decisions and drive your inner beliefs?
- What causes you to smile?

*Step 4: Looking to the future*

- What would you like to achieve by the end of your lifetime? What would you like to be remembered for or have spoken about as your epitaph? There might be any number of achievements from a couple to a couple of dozen. You don't need to be practical.

*Step 5: Setting sail*

- Fast-forward say a dozen years from now. In your ideal life, what are you doing? What are you feeling? Who are you with?
- Try writing this down. Or talk about it with a friend. What do you notice about your excitement/energy/feelings?

## *Activity 3*

The thirteenth-century Persian poet Rumi is credited with saying: 'When you do things from your soul, you feel a river moving in you, a joy.'

- Choose to do at least one of today's activities 'from your soul'. What difference does it make to you? Why?
- Suggest it to some of your coachees and explore their responses. Don't initially define 'soul': most people will

have at least a hazy notion of its meaning. Then, after the activity, ask them about their understanding of 'soul', for example:
  o What do they think it is?
  o What's its purpose?
  o What did they take the activity to mean?
  o What was the impact?
  o How/would it have been different if phrased as 'enjoy today', for example?
- What makes you 'come alive'? (While this may seem a strange question to ask in a business context, what emerges usually unmasks some core values, motivators and behaviours, those things that in combination give us a sense of fulfilment, satisfaction and meaning.) This can lead into an exploration of whether these are currently met at work and if not when/where/why/how they are or might be. When have they been met in the past?

## *Activity 4*

The following questions can be used as and when you as a professional coach feel appropriate:

- Describe your own spiritual beliefs and how they relate to the beliefs of others.
- To what extent do they affect the way you operate at work?
- How do you sustain yourself during difficult times?
- How is your sense of purpose reflected in your work?
- Think about two or three individual experiences at work when you have been lifted to a new level of performance and/or achieved far more than you thought possible. Describe what happened and how you felt.

## *Activity 5*

Discussions about spirituality in work often seem to arise, organisationally, under the 'diversity' label. What are the advantages of this diversity label? What are the disadvantages? What are the alternatives? What are the implications of this for the coach? If a staff member were to be discovered reading a sacred text at work during his or her own time would it be deemed inappropriate or prejudicial or awkward either by the organisation or by the individual?

## *Activity 6*

Listen out for the following trigger comments or those similar and use them as an opportunity to pursue the questions of meaning and spirituality covered in this chapter:

- I feel there's no point.
- I feel empty, lost, disillusioned.
- I feel burnt out, unmotivated or disconnected.

## *Gateway words and phrases from David's coaching sessions*

I suggest the following, though they are by no means exhaustive:

- 'Celebrate what young people could achieve.'
- 'To challenge.'
- 'It really inspired me.'
- 'It makes the hairs on my neck stand up even now.'
- 'There was a sense of purpose about it.'
- 'So that no one else had to go through what I went through, the uncertainty.'
- 'I can almost hear the applause again ringing in my ears.'
- 'I felt I was on a mission to change the world.'
- 'I felt so ashamed.'
- 'I felt I was making a difference, some positive contribution.'
- '(They) seemed to have something that we'd lost.'
- 'They had a sense of meaning in life that I didn't.'
- 'How might my life have been different?'

Choose two examples from my list and explore how you as the coach might prompt SQ. For example, see Table 5.1.

*Table 5.1* Gateway words

| David's words | How the coach might prompt SQ |
|---|---|
| *No one else had to go through what I went through, the uncertainty.* | |
| *I felt so ashamed.* | |

# Part Three

## Skills and resources

# 6

# Developing the coach's skills

**Overview**

## *Health warning*

First, this chapter is not an all-you-ever-wanted-to-learn-about-being-a-great-coach-in-one-easy-chapter. That would be neither appropriate nor possible. Neither is it a comprehensive guide to effective coaching practice. Other books do that far more comprehensively.[1] This chapter simply gives a brief overview of some of the key coaching skills as they might apply in the context of meaning and spirituality.

Second, if this *is* an area that you feel you can cover with professional neutrality irrespective of your personal beliefs (and the fact that you're reading thus far suggests it is), then it's worth considering: 'What is my greatest concern about raising this with clients?' (Make a note of your responses.) Often this will include something about 'religion' – which is one outward manifestation of spirituality – and its reputation as a no-go area in the workplace. Or it might be the fear of accusations of proselytising or making some religions or beliefs 'wrong'. Or of being dismissed as 'soft' or ineffective. Mostly this is an issue about language and terminology rather than about substance. If we return to the definition early in this chapter ('Spirituality is an innate need to connect to something larger than ourselves'), then surely there can be few disagreements about it being an area eligible for exploration.

## Introduction

You are (hopefully) not the only person reading this book. Your fellow readers may be experienced coaches looking to broaden their expertise by considering this emerging area. They may be new coaches with the ink not yet dry on their diplomas. They may be 'religious' people interested in what they might bring to the table. They may be academics and researchers interested in seeing what this important dimension will add to their programmes and courses. Some will simply be curious. Some may come to this chapter first; others may come to it last as a result of having read all the other chapters . . .

The purpose of this chapter is to consider how some key coaching skills operate specifically in this area of meaning and spirituality, to make it a road *more* travelled. If we *are* innately spiritual creatures, facilitating this with our coaches must have a huge positive knock-on effect and hence is ignored by businesses, coaches and individuals only at great peril and loss.

Specifically in coaching terms, let me return to the main definition of 'spirituality' used in this book:

> the way by which people connect the activities of their daily life with their wellsprings of deepest meaning . . . Our innate need to connect to something greater than and external to ourselves – something sacred or divine that seeks to empower me and engage me in transformation of the greater good.

One of the primary functions of coaching is to foster interconnectivity or integration in the lives of the individual so as to raise both their own awareness and their participation in all elements of their life and thus become more effective (however effectiveness is defined). Even if coaches are engaged to deal with just one specific aspect (e.g. business), to ignore the others risks compromising effectiveness and impact. If spirituality is an innate part of who we are then it's vital that coaches at least facilitate the possibility of that voyage of discovery. It is an important quest.

Earlier chapters considered situations where work, work-life (im)balance and crises may trigger in the coachee the opportunity to explore meaning and spirituality. That trigger might be entering a new phase in life. It might be times when attitudes and responses that have hitherto worked perfectly well no longer seem appropriate or adequate. It might be when previous strengths begin to show their shadow side and priorities shift like the sands of the desert, resulting in a profound sense of disorientation. The trigger might be the birth of a baby or reaching a 'significant' birthday. It may even be the emergence of a new generation: both Gen X and Gen Y seem to place a greater interest in and importance on spirituality, for example.

This chapter deals specifically with skills perhaps only implicit in other chapters, skills such as:

- raising awareness: understanding and spotting the opportunities to explore emerging SQ (the measurement of Spiritual Intelligence);
- hearing the unspoken and especially the *style* of language the coachee is using without putting words into the mouth of the coachee;
- identifying the core vocabulary and using it accurately;
- considering the stages of development in both life and spirituality;
- developing the coach's own personal and professional practice relating to coaching in the realm of meaning and spirituality and especially the importance of supervision in this far-from-straightforward dimension.

It concludes with some practical exercises.

## Spirituality

For convenience, coaching is often separated out into areas of specialism such as 'sport', 'business', 'life' or 'executive'. It may be that 'spirituality' is a distinct area of specialism, though on balance I would argue that it is also important in each of the other areas. Most coaches will not be considering 'spirituality' as a specialism in its own right, alongside business coaching, executive, life, sports, etc. And, on the whole, I think that is a positive. Once spirituality is separated out and labelled differently as a 'specialism' it gives the rest of us the perfect excuse to avoid it altogether. I also remain firmly convinced that humans are innately 'spiritual' beings and hence need to develop understanding in that area in order to become fully the person we're called to be. Therefore Spiritual Intelligence (SQ) needs to be part of the toolkit for all coaches, alongside an awareness of EQ, stages of personality and adult development, questioning and listening skills and many more.

In this book I have used the term coaching to refer to a one-to-one context: I am aware that some coaches do undertake what might be described as group coaching. Much of what I have written will apply equally to the group context, though the dynamic web of connections is exponentially more complicated. As I have written elsewhere in this book it's not unusual in a team context for the term 'team spirit' to arise and this could provide the opening for a very illuminating discussion about what is meant by 'spirit' – and what is not. The final section of this chapter contains a far-from exhaustive list of contexts and terminology where it may arise, with a little encouragement and creative thinking.

At this point a reminder: as professional coaches we are committed to work with the coachee's agenda, not our own. Even if spirituality is an area that raises a red mist in us, that does not excuse us from raising the question, though it may mean we recognise our own limitations and pass the answering of it to someone more experienced in this area. That said, one of the specific purposes of this book is to equip *all* coaches with sufficient paradigms, ideas and practical activities to both inspire confidence and provide rudimentary skill; the rest comes with practice, experience and further reading.

In the updated version of the 1980s best-selling book *Build Your Own Rainbow*, the authors Hopson and Scally[2] describe how writing the chapter on spirituality in the new book naturally fell to Mike Scally since he has a strong religious faith, but the further they got the more Barrie Hopson discovered he was also a 'spiritual' being and that this did not require any form of recognisable religious faith. Examining terminology and concepts is both vital and valuably illuminating.

## *Understanding ourselves and others*

There is a famous story of the Greek gods Zeus and Hera observing the plight of mankind from Mt Olympus that has particular resonance in the current economic climate and this context. Zeus' wife Hera was particularly troubled by the sight of an elderly peasant burdened by poverty, hunger and the demands of his family. Hera begged Zeus to help. 'Gladly,' Zeus is described as replying, 'As soon as he's ready.' Hera is indignant and points out it would be simple for the King of the Gods to magic a sack of gold in front of him. So Zeus obliges. Whereupon the peasant carefully steps around the stumbling block to avoid further damaging his decayed sandals.

Part of the role of the coach is to help the coachee differentiate between sacks of gold and stumbling blocks, to discern those things that will leverage fundamental development and those that provide merely an entertaining diversion and to recognise where current focus is blinding or distorting.

But what does that actually mean in practice? In Chapter 1, I briefly mentioned Rashida. As promised, we return to her here, starting with a brief résumé. Rashida is feeling frustrated at work. It's an all-too-familiar story. Her promotion is being blocked by a self-serving manager in an organisation unwilling to listen. The traditional approach is that it's a work-based problem requiring work-based solutions: either her boss or Rashida needs to change or she needs to get out. As coaches, we would draft some questions to help Rashida explore her relationships with her colleagues, how other people experience the behaviour of the self-serving manager and how they experience Rashida, why she thinks the organisation doesn't want to listen, her own role in the organisation, where she'd like to get to in say five years, what she currently finds frustrating, what would need to change. Maybe there are issues around gender, diversity . . . and many more.

Back in Chapter 1, I suggested that this might in fact be hanging our questions onto the wrong hook, that in fact there might be something deeper going on in Rashida requiring us to chip at the layers of the iceberg beneath the surface and look beyond actions and behaviours to the beliefs and values that make Rashida fundamentally Rashida. Let's return to the story at the point of her answer to the question, 'What might set your spirit free?' Rashida's evolving story will provide the ongoing vehicle in this chapter for examining the coaching skills from the perspective of spirituality.

Rashida: *Set me free?* Good grief . . . no idea! Apart from Gerry leaving? I guess the chance to be who I really am, to do what I'm best at. It just seems as if I always have to do what other people want me to do, in the way they want it done. I don't get any *creativity*.

Coach: What might that creativity look like, if you were given the opportunity?

Rashida: The opportunity? I'd run my team completely differently. Draw them in much more, *empower* them but also get them to take responsibility. Give them some *freedom*. Most of them have got some really great ideas but they're never given the chance.

Coach: Why is that important?

Rashida: Well, I guess we're all in this together so it would help us build a good *team spirit*, something we all feel part of. I'm not sure how to put it, I've never really thought about it like that . . .

Coach: What would it take for you to get up and do what needs doing?

(There's a long pause.)

Rashida: You know what? When you asked me that, I suddenly felt – almost a – like, lump in my throat. Like it's something I've really got to do, got no choice in.

(Rashida has suddenly sat bolt upright in her chair.)

It may be that you can hear the voice of one of your coachee or a friend or even your own voice in that of Rashida. Equally, it may be that her words are far away from your own though you might recognise the sentiments behind them.

Different personality types are likely to both approach and express the quest in different terminology. One of the most widely used personality type indicators is known as Myers-Briggs (MBTI).[3] In Myers-Briggs terms, Rashida shows signs of Introverted Thinking typology.

## *Spiral Dynamics*

Spiral Dynamics has an even more detailed presentation of how spirituality is expressed and actioned.[4] Using eight colours (Beige, Purple, Red, Blue, Orange, Green, Yellow and Turquoise) it sets out progressive stages of adult development. To an extent these stages represent a worldview: the secular-scientific outlook is likely to appeal to Orange; traditional religion to Blue/Purple and spirituality to Green. Thus Orange is likely to be sceptical of both religion and spirituality while Blue, Purple and Green may react from a common humanity perspective to what they see as the brutal capitalism, insensitive science and morally neutral medicine that is so attractive to Orange. So for Blue their language and thought patterns tend to be about creating order and purpose out of chaos. For Orange they are about using reason and logic to create a better life for all. For Green it is often social justice, harmony and stewardship of the planet. This does not mean that questions of spirituality won't be of interest or value to, say, an Orange, merely that it will affect the style of language and concepts most likely to be the vehicle by which it is expressed.

### Activity

Which of these three selected types (Blue, Orange and Green) seems closest to Rashida's words?

## *Stages of life and faith*

There is a fuller discussion about the meaning of the term 'spirituality' in Chapter 2. This section explores the idea that Spiritual Intelligence (SQ) is developmental, alongside the other key intelligences (IQ and EQ); this was illustrated in part one of the coaching case study of David in Chapter 2 and Rashida in this chapter.

Countless different writers have dealt with life-stages and the process of self-actualisation in far more detail than is appropriate here: Maslow, Herzberg, Piaget, Freud, Jung: the list is endless.[5]

Sigmund Freud believed that as well as life stages through which we progress as on a journey we also have within our life some areas that we are comfortable to inhabit and others that, rather like rooms in a house, we keep strictly under lock and key from ourselves and from others. In particular we have a basement, a shadowy place where latent drives, urges and unresolved conflicts reside. Some view it as the home of the mind/personality and for Freud it was particularly significant.

Aldous Huxley later suggested that if we can have a basement why couldn't we have an attic too? His idea was that just as Freud suggested the basement as a source for our basic drives, urges and conflicts (hunger, security, sex, hate, etc.) so there could be a source for our higher drives such as love, altruism, artistic and scientific creativity or genius, oneness with nature and spiritual vision, which might be termed an 'upper unconscious' or attic.[6]

So the viewpoint I am following is that humans are innately spiritual beings; yet in the centuries following the ironically named Enlightenment, science, reason and fact have overshadowed and devalued the credibility of spirit and thus caused a distortion. Only as we progress into the twenty-first century is the idea of the spirit beginning to re-emerge as a credible entity. It is stirring like a sleeping giant; or perhaps more appropriately, stretching and developing like a long-neglected muscle.

Like many creatures emerging from a long period of sleep into the bright sunlight again, the initial views are often rather blurred and incomplete. Back in the 1970s American psychologist Lawrence Kohlberg suggested that our sense of moral awareness and the actions thus ensuing was also developmental, progressing through six levels[7] and culminating in our adherence to universal ethical principles. In the 1980s, James Fowler[8] built on Kohlberg's level 6 and suggested a stage 7, the 'god' stage. Fowler argued that his own research suggested that 'faith' itself is developmental.[9]

I am aware that I have suddenly started writing about 'faith' rather than 'spirituality'. Unfortunately to date there's been far more research and academic study of faith rather than of spirituality. So for the moment we draw on the areas of similarity and await further research into the areas of difference; and we do so with caution.

Perhaps more useful at this point in the context of coaching, meaning and spirituality is the work of John Westerhoff.[10] He argued that faith, like the human body, has an expected pattern of growth and development. The different stages are usually addressed at certain ages and can, like physical growth, be delayed or developed depending on circumstances encountered. (Coaches can therefore have a role in helping coachees 'catch up' on their spiritual growth.)

When we left Rashida, she'd just been shocked as her coach asked her what it would take for her to 'do what needed doing . . .' That's where we pick up.

Rashida: Actually, now you've mentioned it, not very much.
Coach: So what's stopping you?
Rashida: I guess I'd never really thought of it as my responsibility.
Coach: Why?
Rashida: Gerry's just not like that. He doesn't like other people doing a take-over.
Coach: Is this the first time you've come across someone like that?
Rashida: No – my first boss was exactly the same. Lots of staff left just during the two years I was there. A real bully.
Coach: Are you willing to tell me what happened?
Rashida: Well, one day soon after I joined, I took an idea to him that I *know* would have made the team happier and more efficient and he tore a strip off me in front of all the others. Said what right did I have as a junior to be telling him how to run his staff. I didn't make that mistake again.
Coach: So are you saying that in some ways, Gerry reminds you of your first boss?

Rashida: Yes. Exactly.
Coach: Which of your skills was your last boss *not* allowing you to use?
Rashida: I think I'm good with new ideas. I like to be able to take responsibility when there's something I feel really strongly about.
Coach: In what way is Gerry different?
Rashida: Actually, in fairness, on a good day he's much more collaborative. He quite likes new ideas. It's just that he's under such pressure he doesn't have time to listen properly. If he's not got it in the first couple of minutes then he just brushes it off. Sometimes it seems as if he's on a different planet!
Coach: A different planet?
Rashida: Yes. We just have completely different outlooks and approaches. And I don't mean he's always wrong, of course. I've actually learned some quite important things from his views.
Coach: A moment ago, you talked about new ideas and about being able to take responsibility for things you feel strongly about. Why is that important to you?
Rashida: Because I believe everyone has a right to be heard about things that they feel passionately about. Especially when they benefit other people as well.
Coach: For example?
Rashida: For example . . . (She pauses to think. Her eyes have become more intense, brighter. She's getting energised – a point not lost on her coach.) For example, a couple of weeks ago I had this great idea to incentivise my team. It would have given them much more control over the work they do and how they do it. It would have been much more interesting for them. Oh – *and* it would be better value for the company! I got really energised by it for a few days, even worked on the idea over a weekend.
Coach: So what happened?
Rashida: Well, I had this great one-sider to explain it. Even a cost-benefit analysis. But when I took it to Gerry, he just dismissed it.

Coach: What exactly did he say?

Rashida: 'I'm too busy to look at that at the moment.' It just killed me stone dead.

Coach: Understandably. But – was he lying to you to put you off?

Rashida: Oh no, don't think so. He *is* really busy at the moment with end-of-year accounts.

Coach: So – if he really was busy, if he wasn't giving you the brush-off . . . ?

Rashida: (She grins.) Something's telling me I probably ought to plan a better moment. Try again. Wow – that's really exciting . . . Maybe I could . . .

Coach: So if you were given free rein in your work what would feed your soul?

Rashida: Actually, that's a really interesting question. When I first left uni I'd seen so many people who seemed to get sucked into the system and I vowed I'd never do that, I'd never compromise my values. I even wrote down a list, things like 'being authentic'. About keeping my inner harmony. Sounds trite now, but . . . Oh, and about being true to my soul and the soul of others . . . I've still got the list somewhere, I'm definitely feeling called to go back to it. Oh my god, how cheesy does that sound! But I will, though. Tonight!

In terms of Wigglesworth's quadrants of SQ (see Chapter 7) Rashida is showing signs of being primarily in Quadrant 2: Universal Awareness (she talks about her feelings of interconnectedness and with her awareness of the worldviews of others) but starting to move into Self and Self-Mastery (with her thoughts about inner harmony and her own spiritual growth, as well as living out her purpose and values).

## *The Corridors of Power*

As Rashida shows, there are many routes that might lead into opportunities to explore spirituality and its impact. In the workplace, these might include:

- diversity
- team building
- stress/resilience
- retention, employer-of-choice status
- work-life balance
- wellness
- morale/motivation
- Emotional Intelligence
- values and values alignment
- social responsibility
- change management
- the quest for inspirational leadership (inspire = in spirit),
- innovation and creativity . . .

This list is not exhaustive. 'Spirituality' is like a room approached via numerous corridors, but a room often blocked off by a curtain behind which we're reluctant to peek.

## Coaching skills

### *What is coaching?*

Most coaches have their favoured definition. My personal definition is that 'Coaching is helping a coachee – through guided questioning and discussion – to solve a problem or perform better than might otherwise have happened and thus be more effective and fulfilled'. By performance I mean not just in the business sense but in the much wider sense of the way they live their life and seek growth for themselves and those around them.

Coaching is therefore concerned with helping people move beyond their present capability, whether that is a physical skill (as in the workplace or on the sports field) or an intellectual one (applying new concepts) or an emotional one (a greater understanding of self, others and impact) or a spiritual one (a greater sense of purpose, interconnectivity and attraction towards a Higher Power). Coaching is unlocking a person's potential to maximise their performance across *all* their aspects. It can be highly effective in business, recreational, social and sporting contexts.

*Table 6.1* **Coaching and similar strategies**

| coaching | mentoring |
|---|---|
| facilitating | teaching |

Coaching is often described as one of a quadrant of similar strategies (see Table 6.1). The distinction between each lies in the balance of input between the parties and where the focus lies. At its extreme, teaching may demand no input whatsoever from the recipient; at the opposite end of the spectrum, coaching may be 80 per cent input from the recipient, with the coach's 20 per cent predominantly question-based. In coaching, the focus remains on the coachee, on drawing out from them that which already lies, often unrecognised, within them.[11] Thus Nancy Kline's famous remark that the brilliant executive coach is the one who brings out the brilliance of the client. Coaching is about unlocking a person's potential to maximise their performance, about learning rather than teaching. It is about thriving in the new learning environment. Contrary to the old 'Behaviourist' assumption that we are 'empty vessels' into which information is 'poured', the newer model suggests we are more like an 'acorn' which contains within it all the potential to be a magnificent oak tree, simply requiring nourishment. The role of coach is as gardener or arborealist.

One of the main benefits frequently ascribed to having a coach is maximising an 'outside' perspective, someone who can stand outside the situation and prompt a wider reflection.

If that is the case the broader the perspective the coach can bring the richer the canvas available to the coachee for exploration. That remains true whatever the primary purpose of the coaching engagement. It doesn't mandate the coach to explore whatever comes up irrespective of the terms of engagement; the coaching goals remain paramount. But they are goals, not straightjackets, and there can be some important corridors to explore en route to them, if I may mix metaphors. Especially in the business arena it can be very tempting to focus solely on the business objectives; but we are humans and not machines so we do not operate in isolation from the rest of our life the moment we cross the threshold of our employment, much as some bosses might wish we did. In fact, it's in the best interests of the business that our coachees bring the best of themselves to work. Given that one of the primary organisational concerns is building and maintaining motivation, which is itself grounded in a sense of meaning and values, where those are not acknowledged, understood and met then performance will inevitably be diminished. Coaching is at its most effective when it refocuses motivation by establishing and maintaining The Balanced Life. In a world where so many live to work rather than work to live the realm of meaning and spirit can make an invaluable contribution by gently highlighting motivation and self-fulfilment and helping coachees move towards their goals in the broadest sense. Hence a fundamental coaching skill is the ability to identify and explore these spheres.

## *Identifying the characteristics of good coaching*

The main characteristics of good coaching include:

- establishing *positive* personal relationships where the needs of the person being coached are placed above those of the coach;
- identifying *purposeful* goals;
- creating *productive* learning environments that extend the coachee and result in changed *behaviours*, attitudes and actions and promote skill development;
- introducing new *perspectives*, horizons and personal challenge;

- discussion and *exploration* rather than telling;
- evidence of *improved motivation*, clarity of vision and performance;
- reinforcing a *culture* of support, challenge, experimentation;
- encouraging *implementation* of the new skills and behaviours and insights and passing them on to others.

In effect, good coaching requires the patience of a saint; the hide of a rhino; the wisdom of an owl; and the interpersonal skills of a debutante. I'll leave the graphic of that to your imagination . . .

This is of course a gross oversimplification since this is not the place to cover in detail. A visit to any bookshop or a careful web search will yield a multitude of books, articles and resources to prompt thinking, learning and, occasionally, incredulity. In my opinion the coach is best served by identifying one main coaching model that has widespread acceptance and then supplementing this with perhaps one or two more available in their repertoire for use when appropriate. In reality most experienced coaches will say that as they gain experience they often blur the boundaries anyway. So as a 'starter' here are five that seem to be a robust fit to the area of spirituality and are easily remembered . . .

## *The GROW Model*

Developed by Sir John Whitmore and now one of the most widely used models for coaching, GROW consists of:

G = Goals: what does the coachee want from this session?
R = Reality: what's *really* going on – as opposed to what's described.
O = Options: the coachee creates 2 or 3 different options, then selects:
W = What they will specifically do as a result of this session and When.

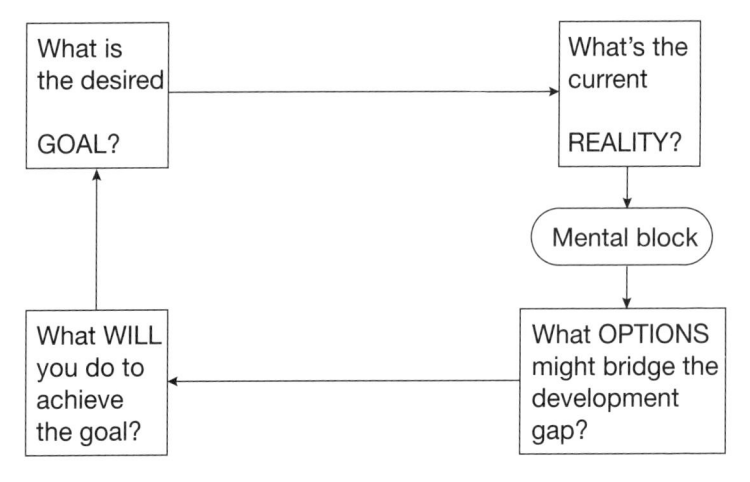

```
┌──────────────┐                    ┌──────────────┐
│ What is      │                    │ What's the   │
│ the desired  │───────────────────▶│ current      │
│              │                    │              │
│ GOAL?        │                    │ REALITY?     │
└──────────────┘                    └──────────────┘
        ▲                                   │
        │                            ( Mental block )
        │                                   │
        │                                   ▼
┌──────────────┐                    ┌──────────────┐
│ What WILL    │                    │ What OPTIONS │
│ you do to    │◀───────────────────│ might bridge the │
│ achieve      │                    │ development  │
│ the goal?    │                    │ gap?         │
└──────────────┘                    └──────────────┘
```

*Figure 6.1* **GROW**

Goals
Goals should be:

- clear;
- located within the person's overall vision or desired future;
- within reach;
- challenging, perhaps differentiating between Dream Goals and Minimum Acceptable Goals;
- stated in positive language, with a positive theme;
- revised if necessary during the next two stages (Reality and Options).

In other words, using the SMART acronym, goals need to be Specific, Measurable, Achievable and Time-bound. In the business context, the coach can often provide a valuable intermediary role in ensuring that the coaching goals agreed with or imposed by the organisation are also SMART.

Reality
What is reality? In some ways this is the most important block in the coaching session. Yet it is the one most often either overlooked or superficially skimmed. It is the point where coaches prompt and prod the coachee to examine

whether the goals they've identified are the keys to unlock and explore or whether they are the mirrors that deflect. Experience suggests that the presenting issue is rarely the underlying cause. In this section coaches normally:

- explore why this is an issue for the coachee;
- draw out the different influences, e.g. people, location, time, power, resources, money, attitudes, rules, etc.;
- explore the perceptions of others involved;
- challenge the coachee's assumptions;
- refine the detail ('You say they're always arguing – how often has this happened in the last week? What was the context?');
- consider the consequences of past actions;
- encourage the coachee to explore below the surface: are there issues of control, power, threat, insecurity, confidence . . . ?

### Options

This is deliberately plural. The temptation is to go with the first suggestion but this is rarely good practice. Encouraging the coachee to generate several and then explore each often results in a much more robust 'first choice' solution and also a viable fallback. In this section coaches normally:

- spend plenty of time exploring 'What if. . .?' questions;
- reserve their own suggestions, at least until the coachee's have dried up – and possibly longer;
- encourage the capture of all ideas;
- identify possible actions from all options including the wild ones;
- explore the strengths, weaknesses, benefits and costs of each, then encourage the coachee to rate each option on a 1–10 scale.

### Will

What the coachee commits to do and when. The more specific these are the more likely they'll be attempted. This also gives the coach the opportunity to consider whether a timely reminder or encouragement might be useful. In this section coaches normally encourage the coachee to:

- commit to at least one option;
- identify the first step;
- write in the diary when that step will be taken;
- determine who they will tell about/involve in the action/s, why and when;
- decide what will constitute successful completion.

Two further points about the GROW model. One of the biggest temptations is to move straight from Goals to Options. The coach needs to probe what is described in order to clarify whether it is the real or the only story. Otherwise this risks generating Options to something that isn't actually the issue.

Another temptation is to generate only one Option, to go with the first suggestion. However, the truism that, 'The first solution is rarely the best solution' is a truism precisely because it's often true.

The GROW model is still the most widely used. But each of the following might also be useful in coaching for meaning and spirituality.

## *The ADAPT Model[12]*

A = Assess current performance.
D = Develop a plan.
A = Act on the plan.
P = Progress check.
T = Tell those who need to know.

This model takes something of a project management approach and can be useful where there are quite specific, defined and limited goals. The crucial area is the first 'A' and I include it here because there is a risk that in very mechanistic environments or cultures 'current performance' is defined solely in terms of technical skills rather than necessarily including the wider performance-inhibitors that meaning and spirituality facilitate.

## *The CO-ACTIVE Model[13]*

This model is represented as a circle encompassing the five points of a star. The star represents the client's trio of

Fulfilment, Balance and Process; the points of the star represent Listening; Intuition; Deepening; Self-management; and Curiosity. It is especially useful when coaching in the area of meaning and spirituality because it focuses on 'what fills the client's heart and soul' and hence impacts all aspects of their life, including work.

## *The CLEAR Model[14]*

- C = Contract clear boundaries and focus for the work.
- L = Listen to words, mood, body language, etc.
- E = Explore what is really happening in order to identify 'A'. . .
- A = Action that will now be taken.
- R = Review the process and agree what next.

## *The EXACT Model[15]*

This model is often used in particular to help coachees identify clear goals that are 'congruent with their own values'.

- Ex = Exciting: a positive goal that acts like a magnet, inspiring.
- A = Assessable: the point that will indicate success (notoriously difficult).
- C = Challenging: coachees tend to under-aim; need to be challenging.
- T = Time-framed: Wilson recommends around twelve weeks on the basis that it takes six weeks to break an old habit and six to establish a new one!

*Excellence in Coaching*[16] outlines a number of other coaching models, including Solution-focused; Cognitive Behavioural; NLP; Integrative; and Transpersonal.

## **Language skills**

### *The need for accurate, agreed language*

It may seem pedantic to keep stressing that 'spirituality' is not the same as 'religion'. But given the symbolic attachment

## 160 SKILLS AND RESOURCES

associated with words it's crucial to be as accurate and precise as possible with terminology. 'Religion', as the outward and organised expression of the beliefs and practices, the dogmas and doctrines, is primarily the domain of church, mosque, synagogue or temple (or the prayer-space within the workplace). 'Spirituality', however, is a more general search for meaning, the sense of connection with the 'higher being' that seeks to empower and engage in transformation of self and others for the broader good.

As I've previously noted, it's my contention that the two main reasons for the relatively slow spread of 'spirituality' as a core competence in the coaching practice have been:

1. The general lack of a commonly agreed and defined spirituality-based terminology.
2. The tendency to avoid it completely in order to avoid potential offence and hence *assume* that it's not a suitable topic, especially for work-based coaching.

Chapter 2 dealt with this in more detail. It also introduced the idea of The Existential Leap – the crisis point when previous paradigms no longer seem sufficient and crumble away into the dust of dissatisfaction and when the abyss of an unknown future seems to loom at our feet. The Existential Leap is a spiritual paradigm and suggests we have two distinct and fundamentally different phases of life: The Warrior and The Elder. The Warrior phase is about the desire to succeed, to establish ourselves and our significant others by delineating our differences from those around us and carving out our unique 'space'. When that created space is subsequently found wanting we face the challenge of whether to accept the current state of dissatisfaction, seek to fill it with other things that themselves then prove similarly dissatisfying or to risk everything by undertaking a fundamental reappraisal. This is the brink of The Existential Leap. If successfully crossed, the new state is that of The Elder characterised by thoughts of legacy, about what of our presence will remain once we no longer exist and what we will be able to put back rather than by how much we can draw out; it is to understand interconnectivity and integration. The Existential Leap lies between the two and not all have the courage to attempt it, especially since abandoning previously accepted paradigms offers no guarantee that there will be a safe landing with new ones. The presence of an experienced coach can make all the difference.

Chapter 1 explained and Chapter 2 developed some *gateway*[17] terms, the use of which might indicate the coachee is engaging with the development of their SQ; a further list appears in Chapter 7.

Finally, I have previously used the image of corridors and rooms where the room represents 'spirituality' that may be approached via a wide range of different 'corridors' and where there is a need to distinguish between the journey and the destination. These are the basic terms that underpin my argument about what spirituality is, why it's so important for the integrated development of the whole person, how this adds value to an organisation and why it's a crucially important area for coaching.

---

### Activity

Look at the lists of gateway and core terminology in Chapters 2 and 7. Which ones do you feel you are most familiar with or understand the best? Turn these into questions that you might use in a coaching situation. Try them out.

*For example*: 'Inspirational': 'Who are the people you find truly inspirational? Why? If someone were to describe you as inspirational, what would you *like* them to mean?'

---

These words provide good clues. But the list is far from exhaustive and the only reliable method is to listen carefully – to the words, the inflection, the context, the body language, the message in the eyes. The coach needs to check with the coachee what they think their words mean and then to help them use these literally as gateways and to 'push' at the door thus presented to see if it will swing open, however creakingly and hesitantly . . .

Enter Rashida once more . . .

Some further background on Rashida's context. She has been with her coach for about 18 months. A banker, she's been promoted to partner because of her success with clients but has found leadership difficult. This has not been helped by the fact she feels unsupported and sometimes undermined by her immediate boss, Gerry. In this next session Rashida is chatting generally with her coach 'before we get down to the real business'. She just happens to mention she's been organising a party as she has a 'significant' birthday looming. Her face clouds briefly and her tone becomes unusually quite sombre. It clearly bothers her. 'No', she finally admits, 'It's what it signifies.'

Coach: And what's that?

Rashida: That list I mentioned before? When I was at uni? I sat down and wrote what I wanted to achieve by the time I was 40. It seemed like a lifetime away. But your question got me thinking and I went back and found the list on my laptop. And do you know what, I've achieved every single one – the lot!

Coach: Why do you seem to feel that's a problem?

Rashida: Because I feel I'm still being called to do so much more, that there's so much more I ought to be doing. So the question is: where next? In the next couple of years, the kids'll be off at university. I've got as far I'm going to here. When I wrote the list I thought I'd just retire and enjoy the fruits of my labour. Do all the things I've put off. But I really don't feel like retiring – so much more I can give. Actually . . . do know what? I'm bored to death!

Coach: Okay, here's a complete 'off-the-wall' question: if you could do just one outstanding thing next and you were guaranteed not to fail, what would you do?

Rashida: Good grief. (Long pause.) I suppose . . . I'd want to do something that would make a difference, something that people would remember me for. Something, I guess, quite – audacious. Something transformational.

Coach: 'Transformational'?

Rashida: Well, at the moment all I really do is make money. Nothing wrong with that – and I do it pretty well. I'm good at it. But I'm not sure I'm *respected* by doing it. I just feel I'm being pulled in a different direction now. I need something that's more in keeping with what I felt called to do. To my values, I suppose.

Coach: You mentioned feeling 'called'. What do you mean?

Rashida: Well, at uni I felt I was being challenged to do something that would help people, to make a difference. That something out there had a greater purpose for my life. And I know I've done that with the kids. But I still keep coming back to that question, I feel that same drive inside. Trouble is – I can't work out what on earth it is I'm supposed to be called to do! Apart from making money . . .

---

**Activity**

Now – over to you. As Rashida's coach and given that she is showing herself at least willing to discuss the subject:

1. What questions would you ask her next?
2. Using Wigglesworth's SQ quadrants (see Chapter 7), where might she currently be? What questions might you ask to help her thinking and understanding move forwards?

I have given my thoughts in the postscript at the end of this chapter.

---

Some of the widely used personality profiling questionnaires give valuable insights into effective choice of language at times of transition – especially MBTI[18] since it is built on the ideas of Jung who was himself very committed to exploration of the realm of spirituality. Less well-known but perhaps even more revealing is SIMA – System for Identifying Motivated Abilities.[19] Especially effective at career- and life-crossroads, its carefully researched use of language as the key to unlock what motivates and satisfies can provide a rich starting point and stimulate a 'light bulb' moment.

The role of the coach then is to act rather like an *illuminator*: to work with the language that is being used by the coachee, to hold it up and reflect it back to the coachee and invite their reflection on what their choice of words, phrases, imagery and ideas indicates relative to the exploration of the (divine) spark that lies within us. It's about uncovering and fanning existing embers.

## Listening skills

Active listening is sometimes described as triple listening; that is, conscious attention to the:

- actual words chosen;
- tones and inflections in which the words are delivered (voice); and
- accompanying body language.

The skill lies in being able to do this while also absorbing the actual information given while also thinking whether there are links and commonality, dichotomies and contradictions. While at the same time taking care to avoid the ultimate coaching humiliation: 'I've just said that!!' It involves listening out for gateway words, phrases and subtle shifts in tone, inflection pace and body language that suggest something deeper going on.

In few other types of coaching is body language and voice as important for listening as in spirituality. When the coachee shuffles in their seat or when you sense their energy or excitement level rising, these are strong hints that something deeper is stirring. When their voice hesitates or speeds up, something else is going on behind the words. Equally, a tensing or even a partial turning away may indicate the need to proceed with caution or even move theme completely. The eyes are especially important and with good reason are sometimes referred to as the mirror of the soul: a glazing-over, a sudden avoidance of eye contact, faster or more frequent blinking all give invaluable signs.

> **Activity**
>
> Make a conscious effort over two separate half-days to listen for all the examples of gateway and core terminology of spirituality in general conversations, however unintentional or unrecognised. Listen as you go through each part of your routine: travelling, at work, in the leisure centre, at the pub, in the street, in the checkout queue, over coffee, on TV, etc.
>
> - Make a list of them.
> - What SQ themes, ideas, concepts or words are most frequently used?
>
> Do the same thing with friends or colleagues but this time rather than just listening, intervene: ask a few open or probing questions.

The bibliography lists several books with important sections on listening skills. Nichols (2009) in particular has a useful section on how effective listening builds communal connectivity; Kratz and Kratz (1995) provide an excellent overview and skills.

## Question skills

It is both deliberate and significant that I've put the section on listening skills *before* the section on questioning skills . . . There are many excellent books dealing with the art of effective questioning[20] and this book is not the place to repeat such detail. Suffice it to say that questions are used because they shift the balance of responsibility from the coach back to the coachee. In this section I give a broad overview from the particular perspective of meaning and spirituality. The most commonly used types of questions are listed in Table 6.2.

However, there are other types of question and the art of effective question-asking is probably the greatest skill a coach can contribute. It is one of the first skills a child learns after the power of speech is unveiled. Incidentally, the child's

*Table 6.2* Common questions

| TYPE | EXAMPLE | USED FOR . . . |
| --- | --- | --- |
| OPEN | *What? How? Why? Where? When?* | Early parts of each coaching section; exploration; information gathering |
| CLOSED | *Require only yes/ no answers* | Information confirmation; checking; focussing; ending |
| PROBING | *Tell me more about. . .* | Deepening discussions; refining information |
| REFLECTIVE | *So what you seem to be saying is . . .* | Summarising; recapping; demonstrating listening; releasing underlying emotions |
| HYPOTHETICAL | *What if you were . . .* | Standing in someone else's shoes; exploring possibilities |
| SILENCE | | Encouraging further/ deeper thought, reflection, initiative-taking |

habit of the persistent and repetitive 'Why?' is also a useful coaching tool encapsulated into The '5 Whys' technique: this suggests asking the question 'Why?' five consecutive times in order to help the coachee discover ever deepening answers by which time they will have reached a core value. Suppose as Rashida's coach I had asked the question, 'Why is this birthday such a significant event for you?' and she had replied, 'Because it's my 40th'. My second 'why' might have been, 'And why is turning 40 so significant an event?'

'Because I've just realised I've now achieved all the things that I listed out at 17 that I wanted to achieve by 40.'

3rd 'why': 'And why is that significant?'

'Because I now have no idea what to do next.'

4th . . . 'Why?'
'Because I've achieved all I set out to do.'
5th . . . 'Why does that matter to you?'
'Because I still don't feel satisfied.'

Then the coaching might continue along these lines: 'What might help you feel satisfied?' (Or, 'Have you ever felt satisfied? If so, what were you doing? Why did that satisfy you? What might you do in the next stage of your life that would bring you closer to feeling satisfied? What's currently missing?', etc.) Had the questions ended with just the first 'Why?' the ensuing sections might have been very different.

Knowing what question to ask, when and in what form of words depends on the type of coaching, the person being coached, the degree of trust reached in the coaching relationship, even the mood or atmosphere on the day. It's predicated on careful listening. It takes both skill and experience.

### *Some effective questions to ask in the search for meaning and spirituality*

- Does it really matter, in the broader scale of things?
- Is there more going on than just the here-and-now?
- What am I called to do?
- Who am I called to be?
- Why do you want them to have faith in you?
- What do you understand by 'generosity of spirit'?
- The Existential Question: When you are fully grown up, what sort of person do you want to be?
- What was the most meaningful part for you?
- What are you passionate about?
- Where does your discretionary effort[21] go?
- When time flies – what are you doing?
- What do you enjoy most about your profession/job/work/life at the moment?
- What one thing would you do if you knew you couldn't fail?
- What one sentence would you *like* each of the following to say about you?
  - Spouse/partner?
  - Closest friend?
  - Worst enemy?

- Boss?
- Daughter/son?

A *Johari Window* approach[22] can also be helpful in formulating questions to explore whether meaning and spirit are relevant. It identifies four dimensions or quadrants of self-awareness or disclosure. The original model lists 55 adjectives (see Box 6.1) from which the person is asked to identify five that most closely align to themselves. Then peers are asked to do the same thing for that person.

### Box 6.1

| | | |
|---|---|---|
| Accepting | Forgiving | Non-judgemental |
| Accountability | Flexibility | Openness |
| Achievement | Freedom | Passionate |
| Advancement | Friendship | Peaceful |
| Adventure | Fulfilment | Personal |
| Affection | Give back | development |
| Authentic | Greater good | Pleasure |
| Belonging | Health | Power |
| Calling | Helpfulness | Purpose |
| Calm/centred | Honesty | Quality |
| Collaboration | Humanity | Recognition |
| Commitment | Humble | Respect for |
| Community | Ideological | individuals |
| Compassionate | Inner harmony | Respect for self |
| Competitiveness | Innovation | Responsibility |
| Co-operation | Inspirational | Security |
| Courage | Integrity | Self |
| Creativity | Intuition | Sharing |
| Destiny | Involvement | Support |
| Diversity | Kind | Spirituality |
| Economic security | Loving | Teamwork |
| Ethical | Loyalty | Trust |
| Faithful | Making a | Visionary |
| Fame | difference | Wealth |
| Family happiness | Meaning | Wisdom |

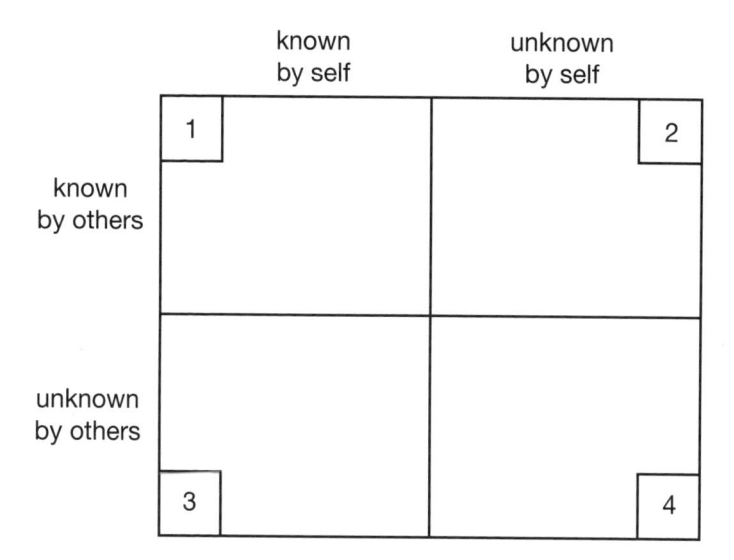

|  | known by self | unknown by self |
|---|---|---|
| known by others | 1 | 2 |
| unknown by others | 3 | 4 |

*Figure 6.2* **Responses**

Responses fall into one of Boxes 1–3 (see Figure 6.2). Box 4 consists of the remainder of the list, i.e. those not selected by either that person or their peers; there can be a useful conversation about whether there were any adjectives from Box 4 they might wish to have seen included and why.

## *Some effective questions based on the GROW model*

These are not in any particular order and are certainly not sequential. I have tried to use examples that open up the possibility for the coachee to consider issues of spirituality. And at this point an important reminder: spirituality is not the same as religion. This is more fully covered in Chapter 2 so here is just a brief reminder of the distinction:

*Spirituality* refers to our innate need to connect to something larger than ourselves – something divine or sacred.

*Religion* is an organised response to human spirituality which usually encompasses a set of narratives, symbols, beliefs and practices ... that give meaning to the practitioner's experiences ... It may be expressed through prayer, ritual, meditation, music and art, among other things.

## *Goal*

- What is your goal for this session?
- How does it relate to your longer-term goals? Vision? Passion?
- What is at the heart of this?
- If you achieve that goal at the end of this session, what does success look like?
- What does success *feel* like?
- How much personal control do you have over your goal?
- What would be a milestone on the way?
- What is a short-term goal on the way? How will you celebrate reaching it?
- When do you want to achieve it by?
- Is it positive, challenging, attainable?
- How will you measure it?
- What about impact?
- On a scale of 1 (low) to 10 (high) how *satisfied* will you feel having attained it?

## *Reality*

- What is happening now?
- Who is involved directly and indirectly?
- When things are going badly, what happens to you?
- How is it different when things are going well?
- If you were to draw a horizontal timeline for the past 10 (or 5, or 15) years, with positive above and negative below, where would you put how you're feeling at this point?
  - How does this compare with twelve months ago?
  - How might it be different in twelve months time?
  - What would have to happen to make it more positive?
  - When you were at your most positive point, what was happening around you?
  - What were you doing?

- How did that feel?
- If you could put a point for the end of your life, how high up the positive
- scale might it be? What would have given you that satisfaction?
- What is currently happening to others directly involved in this situation?
  - What is the effect on them?
  - What have you done about this so far?
  - What results did that produce?
  - What's missing in this situation?
- What do you have that you're not using?
- What's holding you back?
- What is *really* going on?
- What is the person you are called to be?
- To what extent is this moving you towards/drawing you away from your most fulfilling and satisfying goals?
- Where does your motivation come from at the moment? Is it internal? External?
- Are you proud of what you've just described? Why?
- How would the person closest to you describe your reality at the moment?

## *Options*

- What options do you have at this point in time?
- What else could you do?
- If you listened only to your heart (or soul), what feels right?
- What if the ... (time, power, money, authority, etc.) was available?
- May I offer you another suggestion?
- What are the benefits and costs of each?
  - Which will move you closest to your goal/goals?
  - Which will be of most value to other people close to you?
- If you could do just one outstanding thing and you were guaranteed not to fail – what would it be?
- If you followed your head, what would you do?
- If you followed your soul or spirit, what would you do?

*Will*

- Which option or options will you choose? Why?
- To what extent will this meet all your goals? What will you do about any unmet goals?
- What will be your criteria for success?
- What will it not give you? (Do you need a further plan for those?)
- When precisely will you start and complete each step?
- What will hinder you from taking those steps?
- What *personal* resistance, if any, would stop you taking those steps?
  - What will you do to eliminate this?
- Who needs to know what your plans are?
- What support will you need and from whom?
- What will you do to achieve that support and when?
- What commitment on a 1–10 scale will you give these actions?
  - What prevents this being a 10?
  - What could you do or alter to bring it closer to a 10?
- What will your celebration/reward be?

Notice that the verbs are all specific (what *will* . . .) rather than hypothetical or exploratory (what *might* . . .): the aim is concrete, owned actions, date-specific where possible and with clear indicators of both success (scoring the goal) and celebration.

## Professional practice

### *The sound of silence*

In Table 6.2 showing question types I included 'silence'. I am well aware that his may not seem like a type of question at all. But those who have the confidence to use it know it often produces the deepest and most effective reflection and learning. It is a paradox for our professionalism as coaches that the times when our coachees learn the most can be when we say nothing! It may dent our pride – but it may greatly facilitate their development. And this is especially the case when dealing with issues of spirituality; not only is the whole area unfamiliar to many coachees it is also one where language itself can seem inadequate, clichéd or misleading. They need time to think, to pause and to reflect. It is also deeply personal and many might argue that in fact it inhabits the arena beyond words. It is no accident that the deepest mystics often operate in silence and isolation, in a stillness notoriously illusive in the current Western world. The value of silence is partly due to the lack of distraction and external stimuli; it is also partly due to the need to encounter and wrestle with these things internally, deep within our own spirit or soul. For that reason alone (and there are many other reasons) silence can be the most powerful type of question and is therefore an essential part of our professional practice.

## *Fear of failure*

For many coaches the area of spirituality will be as unfamiliar as for the coachee. (Never a bad thing for exploration.) One of the biggest hesitations coaches face is fear of failure. Fear of failure can have all sorts of causes, including success. But at the risk of stating the obvious, certain types of failure are actually beneficial because from them comes the most effective learning that enables both individuals and organisations to innovate and develop more effectively.

A former CEO of Coca Cola once warned his shareholders – and challenged his employees – to fail, because the only way to discover great ideas is to explore ones that fail. Therefore perhaps the only failures that are truly failures are the ones from which the seeds of success are not extracted and replanted. Often when coaches feel uncertain or fearful the temptation is to intervene prematurely before the fruit is ripe. It's a cliché but still worth reminding ourselves that failure can sometimes be success plucked before it's ripe. The skill of the coach is to help the coachee explore when they need to harvest and when they need to garden; to shine light in the midst of 'failure'.

## Continuing professional development

The very fact that you are reading this book indicates openness to further learning. Simply learning more about spirituality itself is important development for the coach; Chapter 7 takes some of the topics and themes raised in this book into a little more depth. But even this can do little more than scratch the surface. The bibliography includes a few from many thousands of possible book titles plus some websites, and an internet search will yield many more. But 'learning' should not simply exist in a vacuum: the challenge is to test it and to put it into practice, so Chapter 7 also contains some suggested resources for using 'spirituality' as part of the coaching practice. The most important thing is to start the learning and then develop with practice.

## Supervision

This is already a vital part of any coach's professional development. I recommend seeking out a supervisor specifically experienced in the area of coaching and spirituality; this is quite a specialised area and having someone more experienced who can act as a sounding board and mentor is important. Again, there are some possible resources in Chapter 7.

## Professional accreditation

There are a growing number of professional bodies either solely dedicated to coaching and spirituality or who include spirituality as part of their banner.[23] Many business schools offer courses that include a consideration of the spiritual and a few coaching consultancies offer training. There are also several LinkedIn groups[24] and other online networking organisations offer similar. They all provide learning opportunities, challenges and validation and should avoid an emerging area of great importance and value being hijacked by the inordinately bizarre or cultishly wacky.

## *A closing word . . .*

Coaching is not a mechanistic functioning of technical skills. It is a relationship. Rapport is fundamental. Without that, no matter how technically competent the coach may be, the actual coaching process will be fatally diminished. Rapport enables coachees to more easily share things about themselves at a deeper level more quickly; they sense that their coach cares about them, is committed to their well-being. The experienced coach knows when rapport is there. And when it isn't there's a strong case for not taking up the coaching contract but drawing in someone else.

> **Activity**
>
> Watch some groups of people in different contexts (work, recreational venue, chatting in the street): which ones seem to demonstrate rapport and which do not? What are the differences, especially in terms of the 'dance' of body language, physical proximity, eye contact, etc.?

## Postscript

Earlier in the chapter there is an activity inviting the formulation of some coaching questions to ask Rashida. Here are my thoughts . . .

For me, Rashida is just beginning to ask questions that show her moving from Warrior to Elder. She starts in Quadrant 3 (Self/Self-Mastery) but is beginning to explore Quadrant 4 (Social Mastery/Spiritual Presence). The remainder of that coaching session might help her explore this new terrain. This particular session draws on a real session that I coached. My questions included:

- May I offer a thought? Maybe it's not about what you're being called to *do* so much as what you're being called to *be*?
- If you listened to your heart or your soul just now, what would it be saying?
- What else? What other options might there be?

- Which options will be of most value to the people who are important to you?
- Which options will set your spirit free? Which will not?

The outcome was that my coachee took one day per week to give investment advice to charities working with the homeless. In his final session he talked with animation about the 'inner harmony' of doing what he'd been called to do, of finding his 'mission in life.' He also remarked with some surprise that other people had started to describe a difference they were noticing in him, saying he was becoming a calming influence; that people were starting to come to him for advice, for his wisdom and insights. At the same time, his boss had asked him to mentor a new entrant.

# 7

# Additional resources

## Overview

This chapter deals with a series of in-depth articles and lists further resources. It is not intended that this chapter be read progressively and sequentially; it does not flow or develop in the way that other chapters do. These articles are included here as an additional resource and for further information about topics, themes and subjects covered more superficially elsewhere in the book and included for those who wish to read about a particular topic in more depth.

## In-depth articles

### *Spirituality*

#### *Spiritual development*

The idea of Spirituality as the fourth Intelligence or Quotient (alongside Physical – PQ; Intellectual – IQ; and Emotional – EQ) is introduced in Chapter 2 and reoccurs with further elaboration in most of the other chapters. For the briefest possible summary here, 'spirituality' is defined as:

> Our innate need to connect to something greater than and external to ourselves – something divine or sacred that seeks to empower and engage me in transformation of the greater good. An activity of the heart and the spirit characterised by words such as 'passion', 'empowerment' and 'legacy'.

SQ is therefore the level of ability of an individual to operate within the dimension of spirituality, much as Goleman and many others have described in the area of EQ. In fact some scholars suggest that SQ is a deeper development of EQ and requires an existing level of competence in EQ.

Developing this idea further, Wigglesworth[1] has proposed four quadrants for SQ similar to those put forward for EQ by Goleman and Boyatzis[2]; there are then 21 (assessable) competencies (see Table 7.1).

Each of these 21 competencies can, she claims, be assessed in 5 levels of skill proficiency. While any of these individual competencies might be present in any type of leader; it is their combination and their context that help produce the spiritually intelligent leader. The role of the coach is to help coachees explore what it means to develop and deploy them collectively in order to make a difference in

*Table 7.1* SQ Competencies

| 1. Self – Self-Awareness | 2. Universal Awareness |
|---|---|
| 1. Awareness of own worldview | 6. Awareness of interconnectedness of life |
| 2. Awareness of life purpose (mission) | 7. Awareness of world views of others |
| 3. Awareness of own values hierarchy | 8. Breadth of time perception |
| 4. Complexity of inner thought | 9. Awareness of limitations/power of human perception |
| 5. Awareness of ego-self and higher self | 10. Awareness of Spiritual Laws |
|  | 11. Experience of transcendent oneness |
| **3. Self/Self-Mastery** | **4. Social Mastery/Spiritual Presence** |
| 12. Commitment to spiritual growth | 17. Wise and effective teacher/mentor |
| 13. Keeping Higher Self in charge | 18. Wise and effective leader/change agent |
| 14. Living your purpose and values | 19. Maker of wise and compassionate decisions |
| 15. Sustaining faith | 20. Calming, healing presence |
| 16. Seeking guidance from spiritual | 21. Being aligned with the ebb and flow of life |

themselves, their staff and their organisation as they become increasingly competent and effective, spiritually intelligent leaders.[3]

## Common traits of a spiritually intelligent leader

What might such a leader look like? What might it feel like to work for one, to employ one or indeed to be one? And is it a good thing anyway? As a result of conversations and interviews with thousands of people about who they admire as spiritual leaders, Cindy Wigglesworth identifies the following common traits of spiritual leaders:[4]

- loving/compassionate/kind
- honest/high integrity/authentic
- humble
- wise
- courageous
- faithful, committed to their ideals
- forgiving
- accepting/non-judging
- calm, centred
- peaceful, non-violent
- passionate
- outstanding teachers
- able to inspire others
- great leaders
- visionary
- persistent in the face of difficulties
- see the gifts inside other people and develop them.

As one writer summarised it, one who is not afraid to deliver the hard messages, one who 'washes the feet as well as applies the whip'.[5]

Like so many analyses of great leaders, once reduced to a list the characteristics look quite mundane. It's their combination both in the person themselves and in their interactions with others that make them stand out. But perhaps above all it's the fact that they are not just their *espoused* values, their aspiration as typically expressed in the CV, but actually their values *in use*, their everyday way of being. They do not come from a set of formulaically learned behaviours or skills but from their core being, their soul. That's not to say that they can't be learnt and honed; but they cannot remain external in a toolkit. They have to be internalised and become unconscious if they are to be recognised as authentic and hence be transformational. They are exercised not because they've been taught that is what a good leader does, nor because they add to the business profitability (though both are true), but because they believe in them. And they continue to operate them whether the organisation is in growth, consolidation or recession and irrespective of whether the leader is under pressure or celebrating success, exercising power or is unseen, going places or sidelined. They join organisations that espouse these values and leave those that refuse to embrace them.

## An incomplete list of gateway terminology

Gateway terminology refers to the use of words that indicate something else may be going on under the surface. Like the best forensic clues, they can easily be overlooked by the 'untrained' eye but if pursued can reveal all sorts of leads towards discovering the broader picture.

| | | |
|---|---|---|
| Accountability | Ethical | Intuition |
| Achievement | Fame | Involvement |
| Advancement | Family happiness | Loyalty |
| Adventure | Flexibility | Making a |
| Affection | Freedom | difference |
| Belonging | Friendship | Meaning |
| Collaboration | Fulfilment | Openness |
| Commitment | Give back | Personal |
| Community | Greater good | development |
| Competitiveness | Health | Pleasure |
| Co-operation | Helpfulness | Power |
| Creativity | Honesty | Purpose |
| Destiny | Humanity | Quality |
| Diversity | Inner harmony | Recognition |
| Economic security | Innovation | Respect for individuals |
| | Integrity | |

| | | |
|---|---|---|
| Respect for self | Sharing | Trust |
| Responsibility | Support | Wealth |
| Security | Spirituality | Wisdom |
| Self | Teamwork | |

Any of these Gateway terms provide a clue that the user *might*, consciously or unconsciously, be asking questions that have wider implications. Of course, they might not. So asking a simple question such as, 'You just mentioned "making a difference": why is that important to you?' or 'When you mentioned "achievement" just now, it sounded as if you were meaning something rather deeper than just your next promotion?' allows for the possibility to emerge and be developed or indicates the need to move on.

Some coaches who are new to this area of coaching keep a list of words or phrases that have triggered this more profound discussion and refer back to it periodically until they become attuned to recognising them when they arise.

## *10 'spirituality' coaching questions*

Great leaders are often inspired by spirituality; their courage comes from their belief in something eternal. Inspired people do exceptional things.

1. What would feed your soul at this point in your life?
2. If you had a month free to help others what would you do? More importantly, why?
3. Describe an occasion when you've felt especially connected to the world around.
4. When have you felt drawn or compelled into a course of action by a greater call? What was the story?
5. When have you felt blessed?
6. If you felt you had a mission in life what would it be?
7. Tell me about a peak experience you've had.
8. What do you think are the spiritual laws of the universe?
9. Who would you describe as today's spiritual leaders? What makes them 'spiritual'?
10. What do you yearn for most, deep down in your soul?

I quote a well-known writer, of particular relevance at this point:

> This is the true joy in life, the being used for a purpose recognised by yourself as a mighty one; the being a force of nature instead of a feverish selfish little clod of ailments and grievances, complaining that the world will not devote itself to making you happy. I am of the opinion that my life belongs to the whole community, and as long as I live it is my privilege to do for it whatever I can. I want to be thoroughly used up when I die, for the harder I work, the more I live. I rejoice in life for its own sake. Life is no brief candle to me; it is a sort of splendid torch that I have got hold of for the moment, and I want to make it burn as brightly as possible before handing it on to future generations.[6]

I recommend typing this quote onto a card (possibly without the source at this point), giving it to coachees and then asking them to comment on what thoughts and feelings it prompts.

In addition the following might also prompt discussion about spirituality *or* meaning:

- What accomplishment are you most proud of?
- What in your life are you happy about?
- What would cause you to resign from your work? Break off a friendship? Terminate a relationship?
- How do you renew your personal sense of purpose and vision?

## *Moral development*

Numerous researchers have examined the field of moral development in individuals or across a community or a society or even (ambitiously) across humanity. But the area of moral development and stages is most often associated with the twentieth-century American psychologist Lawrence Kohlberg[7] at the University of Chicago.

Kohlberg believed that there are six stages of moral development, or more accurately of the development of moral reasoning, and that they are progressively more comprehensive. He felt that there was an underlying principle of 'justice' and that the individual spent literally a lifetime exploring its understanding and application. Interestingly, he felt that regression was very rare. However he later speculated that perhaps there might be a seventh stage which he linked with religion, and that has particular relevance here.

Kohlberg used stories about moral dilemmas in his studies, and was interested in how different people would justify their different actions if they were put in a similar moral dilemma. He then categorised and classified the evoked responses into one of six distinct stages, each with three levels: pre-conventional, conventional and post-conventional.

## Stages

Level 1 (Pre-conventional)

1. Fear and obedience orientation (*How can I avoid punishment?*)
2. Self-interest orientation (*What's in it for me?*)

Level 2 (Conventional)

3. Interpersonal accord and conformity (*The good boy/good girl attitude*)
4. Authority and social-order maintaining orientation (*Law and order, morality*)

Level 3 (Post-conventional)

5. Social contract orientation *(The rights of others)*
6. Universal ethical principles (*Principled conscience*)

Pre-conventional
The pre-conventional level of moral reasoning is especially common in children, although adults can also exhibit this level of reasoning. The morality of an action is judged by its direct consequences for the self.

In *Stage one* (obedience and punishment driven), individuals focus on the direct consequences that their actions will have for themselves. For example, an action is perceived as morally wrong if the person who commits it gets punished. The worse the punishment, the more 'bad' the act. There is no understanding that there might be other perspectives and little challenging of those who administer.

*Stage two* (self-interest driven) is the *what's in it for me* position. Right behaviour is defined by what is in my own best interest. The only interest in the needs of others is the extent to which they might further my own interests.

Conventional
The conventional level of moral reasoning is typical of adolescents and adults. The morality of actions is judged by comparing those actions to those generally held by the society (or subsection of that society) in which one lives.

In *Stage three* (interpersonal accord and conformity driven) the key factor for the individual is approval or disapproval from those around, especially those seen as particularly significant (family, peer group, special interest group, etc.). They try to be a *good boy* or *good girl,* to live up to these expectations, having learned that there is inherent value in doing so. Stage-three reasoning may judge the morality of an action by evaluating its consequences in terms of a person's relationships, which now begin to include things like respect, gratitude and the 'golden rule'.[8]

In *Stage four* (authority and social order obedience driven) it is important to obey laws and social conventions because they maintain a balanced society. Moral reasoning in stage four has moved beyond individual approval; society must learn to transcend individual needs. This often reflects strong commitment to a very few central principles that are described as universal. It can be the domain of fundamentalism. Punishment becomes a significant feature.

Post-conventional
The characteristic of this stage is that now the 'individual' is separated out from 'society' and the individual's perspective takes precedence over the society's.

In *Stage five* (social contract driven), there is a recognition that different individuals hold different and possibly equally valid opinions and beliefs. Laws are therefore regarded as social contracts rather than rigid or universal arbiters of truth. Their function is *the greatest good for the greatest number of people*. This is determined by the opinion of the majority. In this way the concept of democratic government reflects stage-five reasoning.

In *Stage six* (universal ethical principles driven) moral reasoning is based on abstract reasoning using universal ethical principles. Laws are valid only insofar as they are grounded in the overriding principle of justice (defined by common consensus); where they are not there is an *obligation* to disobey those laws. In this way one acts *because* it is right, and not because it is expected or the law. It appears that people rarely, if ever, reach stage six of Kohlberg's model.

## *Further stages*

As his research grew, Kohlberg came across some people who seemed to have undergone moral stage regression. However, Kohlberg responded by introducing the idea that there were in effect sub-stages where the individual was in transition between the major stages. Kohlberg felt this was especially true when transitioning from stage four to stage five (stage 41/2 or 4+ and sharing characteristics of both).

Kohlberg further speculated that a *seventh stage* may exist (Transcendental Morality or Morality of Cosmic Orientation) which would link religion with moral reasoning. However, because of Kohlberg's difficulty providing empirical evidence for even a sixth stage he emphasised that most of his conjecture towards a seventh stage was theoretical.

## **Faith development**

Throughout this book I have assiduously battled to distance 'spirituality' from 'religion'. I have not mentioned 'faith', mainly because it might accurately but confusingly apply to both. However I now need to do so. The reality is that when it comes to questions about development, with the notable exception of Wigglesworth and a handful of other scholars, most academic research so far has been conducted in the realm of religion and *religious* faith. To the extent that 'religion' might be considered one outward and organised expression of something internal and much deeper (with 'spirituality' a different expression but sharing some of the same roots) then there can be much to learn from research into the stages of faith development.

James Fowler,[9] for example, argued that there are seven stages of faith development, which roughly align with chronological or psychological stages of development, though development might be arrested at any stage and often is at Stage 2 (see Table 7.2). However, rather like a neglected muscle, later activity can rapidly catch up and restore it to full use.[10]

*Table 7.2* **Fowler and stages of faith development**

**Stage 0** *Primal* **or** *Undifferentiated* **faith**
Overriding need for safety and warmth; the extent to which the infant feels able to trust and depend on parent/s and other caregivers will colour future understanding of the characteristics of the Divine Being.

**Stage 1** *Intuitive-Projective* **faith**
The emergence of language. Story, symbol and dream become important, with little differentiation between fact and fantasy. If the Stage 0 experiences have, for example, left the child with strong feelings of guilt or of worthlessness, 'God' may be constructed as a taskmaster requiring correct performance in order to qualify for approval and love.

**Stage 2** *Mythic-Literal* **faith**
concrete operational thinking: logic, cause-and-effect and differentiating interpretations. 'God' is seen in terms of rewarding Goodness and punishing Badness. However with the emerging realization that bad things happen to good people many give up and their faith development remains stagnated at this stage.

**Stage 3** *Synthetic-Conventional* **faith**
Conformity and the exploration of meaning. God is invested with those things that are of personal importance: loyalty, understanding and accepting love, support in times of crisis. *But* the overriding impact of what significant-others believe may leave the adolescent frozen in their belief formation by what Fowler calls the 'Tyranny of the They'.

**Stage 4 *Individuative-Reflective* faith**
The recognition of ambiguity; often indicates a disparity between the different elements of developmental growth: their cognitive development may, for example, run ahead of their emotional development so that they become over-confident and unaware of their impact. Religiously, this might be manifested in the attractions of Fundamentalism or of authoritarian leaders. However, lack of awareness of their own unconscious processes can often result in emotional burnout, especially if what is being 'maintained' is a false-self. Fowler describes it thus: 'The wear and tear of maintaining personal boundaries without access to the "heart" they suppressed in adopting the parental or cultural program'.

**Stage 5 *Conjunctive* faith**
Rejoining of things previously understood as being separate; concedes that the confidence of Stage 4 was based at least in part on incomplete self-knowledge. Faith at this stage is about learning to maintain the tensions between multiple perspectives and paradoxes.

**Stage 6 *Universalising* faith**
Back towards reintegration, recognition of universal interconnectedness or what some might call 'enlightenment'. It is the landing on the other side of The Existential Leap.

---

John Westerhoff[11] argued for four distinct stages, usually addressed at certain ages but which can, like physical growth, be delayed or developed depending on circumstances encountered. His stages are:

- *Experienced faith* (preschool and early childhood): imitating actions without understanding the meaning. 'This is what *we* do. This is how *we* act.'
- *Affiliative faith* (childhood and early adolescent years): belonging to a group which still centres around imitating what the group does. 'This is what *we* believe and do. This is *our* group/church.'
- *Searching faith* (late adolescence): asking the question, 'Is this what *I* believe?' This stage of faith is adding the 'head' to the 'heart' of the earlier stages. The answer to the question will either move the individual on to the next

stage or leave them with their development halted, frozen into a shape that will be at variance with their ongoing development in the other intelligences (intellectual, physical and emotional). This is the level when most cult groups recruit their members.
- *Owned faith* (early adulthood): for those who, having explored, now answer: '*This is* what *I* believe!' It is willingly embraced and its effect will impact the remainder of their life in some shape or other.

This section is summarised in Table 7.3.

## *Spiral Dynamics*

Numerous writers in the domain of Spiritual Intelligence draw extensively on the area of Spiral Dynamics.[12] This is not the place to attempt a full description and others[13] do it far more effectively. However, here is the briefest of summaries to give a flavour of its relevance. Its originator seems to have been Clare W. Graves and his name and ideas are then linked with Christopher Cowan and Don Beck.

Spiral Dynamics argues that human nature is not fixed but is a product of nurture, an adaptation made to life circumstances and the emerging, developing understanding of the world. It argues that each new stage both embraces and expands on the previous. This is done via Memes: systems of core values that affect both individuals and whole societies. Each stage is represented by a specific colour. Importantly, neither individuals nor cultures fit into just one colour but are mixtures with differing degrees of intensity. These may also vary over time due to changing life circumstances (think of the ebb and flow of tides) while previous stages also remain available to draw on. The colours intentionally alternate between cool and warm colours. Graves argues that there is no one superior form above all the others but that as conditions in a society change over a period of time one 'colour' may no longer be the most effective representation for that culture and so a new, more effective one is adopted. However, Graves does argue that over a longer period of time higher tiers are better than lower levels. A number of explanations

*Table 7.3* Faith development

| Levinson and Life stages | Childhood and Adolescence | | | | Early Adulthood | Mid-Adulthood | Late Adulthood |
|---|---|---|---|---|---|---|---|
| Kohlberg and Morality | 1. Fear | 2. Self-Interest | 3. Conformity | 4. Social Order | 5. Rights of Others | 6. Universal Principles | Stage 7' |
| | Pre-conventional | | | Conventional | | Self-accepting | |
| Fowler and Faith Development | 0. Primal Faith | 1. Intuitive-Projective Faith | 2. Mythic-Literal Faith | 3. Synthetic-Conventional Faith | 4. Individuative-Reflective Faith | 5. Conjunctive Faith | 6. Universalising Faith |

of Spiral Dynamics give 'ages of history' to the different stages, which are included here.

*Tier 1*

1. *Beige* (From 100,000 BC; Stone Age): dominated by animalistic basic survival; people group together simply because that offers better chances of survival. Famine may reintroduce this stage. (1 per cent of world population).
2. *Purple* (From 50,000 BC; magical-animistic): occurs with the emergence of rites and rituals to appease the spirit and respect clan rule and leaders. Change can only come via the rituals (e.g. reading the bones) (10 per cent of world population – though perhaps only 1 per cent of power).
3. *Red* (From 7,000 BC; exploiting power for self interest): often harsh and dictatorial, as in gangs or the exploitation of slavery/unskilled labour and with a strict division between those who benefit and those who do not. High emphasis on 'heroes' or 'the boss'. (20 per cent population; 5 per cent of power).
4. *Blue* (From 3,000 BC; external authoritarian and patriotic): the social group defines truth; the individual sacrifices self in obedience to authority in order to attain the greater good. The main search is to create order and purpose out of chaos. Authority structures are hierarchical but usually consistent and public (e.g. legal punishments such as flogging carried out in public). In the workplace its manifestation is in clear rules, practices and procedures and 'ethics' is defined in terms of following the rules or the guidance of an expert. Beck argues that Blue industrial practices have moved from America to places like Mexico and Taiwan and will eventually move to Africa. (40 per cent of population; 30 per cent of power).
5. *Orange* (roughly AD 600/1,000; scientific/strategic): rational self-interest is encouraged in order to reach goals, providing it doesn't arouse opposition from those in authority. The use of logic and reason to create a better life. In business the motivators are seen as individual perks and bonuses rather than in group loyalty; competition leads to better productivity and therefore growth. Risk is encour-

aged in pursuit of innovation and growth; 'ethics' is defined as ' don't break the rules – but find the loopholes'. Probably the dominant outlook in the Western economies currently. (30 per cent population, 50 per cent power).

6. *Green* (From 1850; egalitarian, communistic): personal growth and equality sits alongside environmental concern; what one gives is as important as what one receives, trust is valued and disapproval or criticism feared. The role of the leader is to be inclusive, embracing and facilitative rather than heroic, authoritarian or dogmatic. 'Ethics' is defined in terms of following the spirit of the law, doing what is caring. 1960s hippies; Ben & Jerry's ice cream. (10 per cent population; 15 per cent power).

Graves argues that Orange and Green predominate in the (current and Western) workplace.

## *Tier 2*

This involves moving away from the primary focus of subsistence-concerns towards 'being'. However, Cowan parts company with Spiral Dynamics founder Graves at this point, claiming it is a false distinction and that there is no evidence for a second tier or for either Yellow or Turquoise, but that they are simply more complex forms of Orange and Green. Others argue that because Spiral Dynamics assumes ongoing development, further stages are bound to evolve even though in their earliest emergence their characteristics will neither be clearly distinct from their derivative nor fully formulated in their new iteration.

7. *Yellow* (From 1950s; self-expression and avoidance of harm to others): learning is valued in its own right; change is welcomed and there is emphasis on understanding how the parts fit into the overall complexity (systems thinking). Yellow thinkers often 'sit' at the periphery of organisations (to get a better 'view') but have impact by demonstrating that, when integrated, the whole is greater than the sum of the parts. (1 per cent population; 5 per cent power).

8. *Turquoise* (From 1970s; sacrificing self-interest into the holistic greater good in order to achieve integrated

benefit): emphasis on spiritual connectivity. Emphasises that life is more than work and needs balance; drawing down collective intelligence and power in order to problem-solve. Still emerging. (1 per cent population; 1 per cent power).

Importantly for coaches Graves argues that people may be *open* (capable of moving into the next dimension); *arrested* (capable of moving but hindered from doing so); or *closed* (frozen in a current meme). Each requires a different approach, as does the coaching language used with each colour.

Thus *Turquoise* (sometimes called Alchemist or Magician) have the ability to regenerate themselves and their organisations in significantly different ways that are directly relevant to what is needed. They can be characterised by recognition of the interconnectivity as one integrated whole. There is no separation or distinction between 'spirit' and the rest of 'life'. Spirituality is a part of everything and vocabulary often includes 'intuition', 'integration', 'transcending'...

For Yellow (the strategist) there is a dawning awareness that there is truth (and limitations) in all the other previous levels. The drive and hence vocabulary commonly centres around making a difference for the whole (community, society, world). It is acceptable for individuals to believe what they want to believe providing those beliefs do not threaten or damage the collective good.

For Green (the individualist and often called the postmodernist) social justice issues prevail, linked to cultural sensitivity: all perspectives have some truth in them. Vocabulary is around 'justice', democracy', 'rights' and 'equality'...

For Orange (the achiever) thinking and hence vocabulary is focused on the idea that you get what you earn in life and is around 'merit', 'reward', 'competition', 'targets'...

For Blue (the expert) this is characterised by notions of self-sacrifice or obedience to the Common Good/God/Authority Figure. Needs clear rules and autocracy (or in religious terms, theocracy and hence is more prevalent in dogma-centred religions or groups within a religion). Tends to stress the link between right actions/behaviours and hence reward.

For Red (the opportunist) the value is in breaking the rules (or at least in freedom from them) so 'power' is respected and power-based words, phrases and symbols predominate. Life is a 'battle to be won'; 'seize the moment'; 'beat them or they'll beat you'. Often associated with adolescence but some adults do not pass beyond this stage; nor do some religious and political groups.

For Purple (the impulsive) the world is a dangerous place so safety comes through belonging to a group: family, cultural subgroup, religious group, so specific rituals are needed in order to keep safe. People who are firmly in this group (as opposed to transitioning to Red) will typically talk of the 'power of the ancestors', the 'ancient ways'. . .

The final group, Beige, is generally believed to no longer exist in its pure form except, perhaps, in babies because of its pure instinct-driven drive for survival.

There are significant implications for the leader who wishes to develop their SQ. Graves, Beck and Cowan all agree that Tier 2 leaders demonstrate a paradigm shift by being less fearful, more creative in their thinking and faster in their responses so that they create more possibilities.

Tier 2 leaders have a broad concept of time; they may well speak of their 'legacy to future generations'; they are aware of the need to care for the planet for generations to come and will have cultural affinity with organisations that have a long and illustrious past. They can operate at the short-term level but relate this to longer-term implications. They are also aware of the need for 'meaning' for themselves and others. They are not the only group to appreciate this but Tier 2 leaders also have the wider perspective and longer-term view in mind. Being committed to interconnectivity, they are able to stand back and observe for periods of time rather than feeling the need to control or do; they are literally 'going with the flow' yet have the acute sensitivity to also know when to provide the slight 'steer'. They may emphasise 'being' rather than 'doing' and are outstandingly successful. In SQ terms these leaders have the ability to motivate, inspire and bring meaning while still themselves remaining peacefull. They act with love, concern and compassion and are usually described as possessing 'wisdom'.

There is a sense in which these stages represent our worldview: the secular-scientific outlook is likely to appeal to Orange; traditional religion to Blue/Purple and spirituality to Green. Thus Orange is likely to reject both religion and spirituality while Blue, Purple and Green may react against what they see as brutal capitalism, insensitive science and morally neutral medicine that is so attractive to Orange. In some cases the sense of Blue alienation is leading to increased demand for religious government (e.g. Iran) or for 'war' against the secular (Orange) world.

## *Mindfulness*

'Mindfulness is the state of awareness in which we are conscious of our feelings, thoughts and habits of mind, and able to let unhelpful ones go so that they no longer limit us.'[14]

It has long been associated with Buddhism and the conscious control of the mind to concentrate only on those things deemed to be helpful. In Western psychiatry it has begun to be used in a different format as a way of dealing with stress, anxiety and depression. In meditation it is the recognition that 'thoughts' come with messages or interpretations attached which may or may not be accurate; by detaching the thought and its interpretation, new 'meaning' may be found. For example, walking home from the train station in the rain may be associated with 'It's cold, I'm wet and tired and I'm longing to be home in the warmth'. Or, it may be associated with a washing away of the stresses of the day, a time of cool refreshment in preparation for the evening ahead.

Increasingly it is being used rather more mechanistically as a way of becoming more fully focused both in the present and in the process for achieving one's goals: living life with purpose and engaging personal empowerment to start and finish each plan.

It is in the initial sense, the more meditative and reflective sense, that it links especially into SQ. For example, research into spirituality in the caring professions by Martsolf and Mickley[15] highlighted the following key terms for Mindfulness:

- Meaning and the significance of life: the need to make sense of situations and derive purpose.
- Values, beliefs, standards and ethics that one not only holds but which are powerful motivators for actions.
- Transcendence: the awareness and appreciation of a 'transcendent dimension' to life beyond self.
- Connecting: increased awareness of what I have here called connectivity with self, others, Nature/Higher Power and possibly the divine.
- Becoming: a gradual unfolding of life that calls for reflection and experience; it involves a sense of who one 'is' and how one knows. It is similar to what I have called The Existential Leap.

These are all terms that appear more than once in the course of this book and are of great significance for coaching.

## The Johari Window

The Johari Window is a tool that was created in the US in the mid-1950s by Joseph Luft and Harry Ingham (hence Jo-Hari). It was designed to help people better understand their personal impact and communication style.

The subject is given a list of 55 adjectives and picks five or six that they feel describe their own personality. Peers of the subject are then given the same list and each pick five or six adjectives that they feel best describe the subject. These adjectives are then mapped onto a grid.

Charles Handy developed this concept into the Johari House with four rooms (see Figure 6.2). Room 1 is the part of ourselves that we see and others see. Room 2 is the aspect that others see but we are not aware of. Room 3 is the most mysterious room in that the unconscious or subconscious bit of us is seen by neither others nor ourselves. Room 4 is our private space, which we know but keep from others.

Adjectives that are selected by both the participant and his or her peers are placed into quadrant 1. This quadrant represents traits of the participant of which both they and their peers are aware.

Adjectives selected by the participant but not by any of their peers are placed into quadrant 2, representing information about the participant of which their peers are unaware. It is then up to the participant whether or not to disclose this information.

Quadrant 3 consists of adjectives that are only identified by their peers. These represent information of which the participant is not aware, but others are: 'blind spots'.

The remaining adjectives sit in the remaining 4th Quadrant: behaviours or motives which were not recognised by anyone participating.

The 55 adjectives of a Johari Window:

- able
- accepting
- adaptable
- bold
- brave
- calm
- caring
- cheerful
- clever
- complex
- confident
- dependable
- dignified
- energetic
- extroverted
- friendly
- giving
- happy
- helpful
- idealistic
- independent
- ingenious
- intelligent
- introverted
- kind
- knowledgeable
- logical
- loving
- mature
- modest
- nervous
- observant
- organised
- patient
- powerful
- proud
- quiet
- reflective
- relaxed
- religious
- responsive
- searching
- self-assertive
- self-conscious
- sensible
- sentimental
- shy
- silly
- spontaneous
- sympathetic
- tense
- trustworthy
- warm
- wise
- witty

A *Nohari window* is the inversion of the Johari window and is a collection of negative personality traits instead of positive.

| | | |
|---|---|---|
| violent | loud | impatient |
| insecure | self-satisfied | panicky |
| hostile | over dramatic | smug |
| needy | unreliable | predictable |
| ignorant | inflexible | foolish |
| blasé | glum | cowardly |
| embarrassed | vulgar | simple |
| insensitive | unhappy | withdrawn |
| dispassionate | inane | cynical |
| inattentive | distant | boastful |
| intolerant | chaotic | weak |
| aloof | vacuous | unethical |
| irresponsible | passive | rash |
| selfish | dull timid | callous |
| unimaginative | unhelpful | humourless |
| irrational | brash | |
| imperceptive | childish | |

## Further resources

The following have proved useful sources of information for this book, though as always I as the author bear the responsibility for what I've done with it!

### *Organisations*

*Association for Spirit at Work* (www.spiritatwork.org): Although organisationally-dormant, the site still has excellent resources and links.

*Center for Visionary Leadership* ('helping people develop the inner, spiritual resources to be effective leaders') has some useful articles especially about spirituality in business and politics (www.visionarylead.org). There is also a useful article by co-founder Corinne McLaughlin on 'Spirituality and Ethics in Business' that, although sometimes drifting in and out between spirituality and religion, makes some important links with business and leadership performance: www.visionarylead.org/articles/spbus.htm

*Foundation for Workplace Spirituality* (www.workplacespirituality.org.uk): a not-for-profit organisation dedicated to raising spiritual awareness and consciousness in the workplace amongst employees, managers, leaders, the media, shareholders and other stakeholders. Their website contains useful resources, contacts and links for those exploring workplace spirituality.

*Institute for Management Excellence* (www.itstime.com) also looks at spirituality in the workplace and defines it using Seven Principles: Creativity, Communication, Respect, Vision, Partnership, Energy and Flexibility (www.itstime.com/rainbow.htm).

## *Training*

Training in the areas of spirituality is offered by several groups, including:

- *The Coaching Academy*: http://www.the-coaching-academy.com (UK)
- *Conscious Pursuits Inc*: www.consciouspursuits.com (Cindy Wigglesworth – USA)

## *Professional bodies*

*Foundation for Workplace Spirituality* runs conferences and has a good resources section dedicated to 'raising spiritual awareness and consciousness in the workplace amongst the many different stakeholders': www.workplacespirituality.org.uk

*International Association for Spiritual Coaching* (www.joiniasc.org): dedicated to bringing the power of 'spirit' into all aspects of life and humanity's work in the world through 'Spiritual and Transformative Coaching'. They provide resources for 'the art and science of spiritual living and conscious evolution' through research, advocacy and specialised services.

*International Center for Spirit at Work* is a membership organisation that 'supports people who are interested in the integration of spirituality and work'. Though currently dormant, it has some useful resources: www.spiritatwork.org

## *Supervision*

The following UK bodies all offer supervision for coaches and claim to recognise the area of 'spirituality'. The list is far from exhaustive and inclusion here must not be taken as endorsement. They are here merely to give a flavour of what to expect: coaches must undertake their own research and find a supervisor who is both fully accredited *and* with whom they feel rapport.

- Ashridge Business School: http://www.ashridge.org.uk/website/content.nsf/wCOA/Supervision?opendocument
- Association for Coaching: http://www.associationforcoaching.com/dir/ACSupervisors1004.pdf
- Coaching at Work: http://www.coaching-at-work.com
- Foundation for Workplace Spirituality: http://www.workplacespirituality.org.uk/search/node/supervision
- Oxford Brookes University: http://www.business.brookes.ac.uk/futures/cam/CoachingSupervision.asp

## Biography of a Cheshire Cat: Why me?

In the book *Alice's Adventures in Wonderland* a confused Alice seeks directions from the Cheshire Cat, who answers that it depends on where she wants to get to. Whereupon Alice replies that she doesn't much care as long as she gets somewhere. And of course she gets the obvious reply, 'Oh you will – if you go far enough'!

In a way that might summarise my life and career to date. For much of it I've not necessarily been totally clear where I've been heading. I'm not one of those people who while they were still in short trousers fixed on a goal in life and single-mindedly pursued it until it was grasped and held aloft in a triumphant fist! The middle distance has often only emerged slowly out of the very definite mists of time; the long term has usually been the unknown land of uncertainty that the early cartographers dismissed as: 'There be dragons!'

On the other hand neither am I one of those people who seem to drift loosely through life, meandering aimlessly wherever the whim or tide chooses to take me. I've had at least four different careers; but links there have certainly been, though I was not necessarily aware of them at key times; they were not conscious determinants in my decision-making. Perhaps I might say I've worn myriad hats, often at the same time. So if I was wearing a 'spiritual' hat, I might be tempted to say that there was some kind of divine hand guiding me; if I was wearing a psychology hat, I might say I am subconsciously attracted to helping people, making a difference; and if I wore a consultancy hat I might say I'm devoted to change, dissatisfied with status-quo and love innovation.

In the last few years as I've noticed my work burgeoning in the area of coaching, both those I'm working with and for myself, I've found myself increasingly returning to the question that so perplexed Alice. You might argue (with some justification) that this is simply part of reaching the middle of my sixth decade. And that would certainly be true.

But actually, since I notice this increasing amongst my coachees and I coach people from 20s through to 50s, it's not the *whole* story. And 'story' is a central theme in this book, just as the importance of stories is receiving increasing recognition in Western culture. Other cultures, of course, have never lost sight of their importance and significance.

Ask almost anyone almost anything and the answer is likely to come back as a story. It seems to be our instinctive way of making sense, of making connections. It is a trait as old as human history, as old as pictures and probably at least as old as language itself. Stories resonate deep within our soul and for millennia have been our link with that something greater than ourselves, the sense of the spirit or the divine.

But it's not just the professional experience in coaching that's brought me to the point of this book. For the 30+ years of my employed life I've been interested in exploring and challenging new ideas, first as a teacher in UK secondary schools (yes, it is possible to teach in England *and* explore and challenge!). Then my journey took a very unexpected twist, leading me to further challenge and explore as an ordained minister in the Church of England for 12 years (yes – it's possible there, as well). Following this, a convergence of numerous issues such as completing a time-bound contract, the break-up of my first marriage and the offer of shared accommodation with a friend, thrust me into embarking on self-employed consultancy as a trainer-facilitator. And apart from a brief two years or so back in full-time employment that brings me up to the current point of Post-conventionalism! (Kohlberg 1976).

Have I always been aware of a spiritual dimension to life? The answer is probably yes. Certainly I have always been involved in that outward expression of it that we term 'religion' – though even that has been a long and sometimes tortuous journey, a relationship of challenge and change rather than a love-affair. Certainly I have usually felt there was some purpose to what I was doing, even when that wasn't necessarily clear to me. I have also felt that there was some form of guiding hand or whispering voice: how else can I explain the opportunities that have come along unbidden yet opportune and relevant?

That, of course, is fine for me. But what about other people? Is this element of spirituality a universal or simply for the lucky chosen few? Many writers would indeed claim it is a universal, not least the psychoanalyst Jung, who believed it vital for a fully formed life. In my role as a Christian priest I have often been in contact with people who would never willingly darken the door of a church nor remotely class themselves as 'Christian'. Yet even through a chance conversation in the street or the pub, never mind the infinitely more likely context of a crises of bereavement or relationship breakup, they have shared with me times when they have felt the closeness of something external and greater. Often they have lacked a vocabulary to fully articulate it, but I have met few who claim never to have experienced any sense of the spiritual or the divine.

It is with the support of some leading Western scholars and researchers and with support from my own experience, therefore, that I conclude that a sense of spirit is indeed inherent to humanity. Eastern thought would be amazed it would even be questioned. If it is a part of who we are, then it has a place right in the centre of everything we do: work, leisure, relationships. And since I am a professional coach that must be part of what I at least offer to my coachees as I seek to serve and challenge them.

Peter Hyson<br>September, 2012

# Notes

## Chapter 1

1 John Donne (1624) *Devotions upon Emergent Occasions.* Meditation XVII.
2 Cindy Wigglesworth. Deep Change, Inc. www.deepchange.com
3 2009 Sherpa Executive Coaching Survey, p. 4.
4 Harman and Hormann, quoted in C. Michael Thompson (2000), p. 6.
5 *Coaching at Work*, Vol. 3 Issue 6, pp. 22–7.
6 See Chapter 4.
7 Contribution from John Whitmore in Wilson (2007).

## Chapter 2

1 David Ellison, quoted in *Time Magazine*, '10 Ideas that are Changing the World', 23 March 2009, p. 31.
2 Bolles (1970).
3 Film in which the main character discovers he has been living his life in a sealed 'movie set' as the unwitting star of a reality TV show.
4 See: www.managementlab.org/future (accessed May 2008).
5 Quoted in E. Cox, Oxford Brookes University Business School. Paper presented to the EMCC UK Conference, 25 March 2008, p. 2. Emphasis mine.
6 Hughes (1988), p. 3.
7 Most notably Strauss and Howe in their 1991 book, *Generations: The History of America's Future, 1584 to 2069*.
8 There is an excellent similar activity around life values in Hopson and Scally (2008) *The Rainbow Years*.

9 If they really do struggle, there's a short list at the end of this chapter.
10 Knight (2003), p. 48.
11 Wigglesworth, C., Deep Change, Inc., www.deepchange.com
12 Author of *The Hitch-hiker's Guide to the Galaxy*.
13 Concentration Camp survivor and author of *Man's Search for Meaning*.
14 Creator of the Hierarchy of Needs for human development.
15 Early twentieth-century psychiatrist specialising in personality disorders.
16 Thompson (2000), p. 31.
17 Probably the best explanation is found in Herzberg's (1968) article, 'One more time: How do you motivate employees?'.
18 Haughey, J. C. (1989) *Converting Nine to Five: A Spirituality of Daily Work*. New York: Crossroad.
19 For an introductory exploration of transpersonal, meaning and spirit from the journal *Training & Coaching Today* (Sept 2007) see: http://www.performanceconsultants.com/img/transpersonal.pdf or in Wikipedia: http://en.wikipedia.org/wiki/Transpersonal_psychology (accessed October 2012).
20 *Coaching at Work*, vol. 3, Issue 6, p. 31; available online at: www.coaching-at-work.com (accessed October 2012).
21 Robert Wuthnow, cit. Reeves in *Management Today* (August 2006).
22 These ideas are based on several sources, e.g. Clare W. Graves, in his article, 'Human Nature Prepares for a Momentous Leap', *The Futurist*, April 1974; the writings of Soren Kierkegaard; and the Gail Sheehy novel, *Passages*. Responsibility for interpretation is entirely my own.
23 See Part 2 of this chapter.
24 Zohar and Marshall (2004).
25 J. A. Conger and Associates (1994) *Spirit at Work: Discovering the Spirituality in Leadership*. San Francisco, CA: Jossey-Bass, p. 17. Emphasis added.
26 See, for example, Wigglesworth: www.deepchange.com (accessed October 2012).
27 King, U. (2004) 'Feminist and eco-feminist spirituality', in C. Partridge (ed.) Encyclopaedia of New Religions: New Religious Movements, Sects and Alternative Spiritualities. Oxford: Lion Hudson.

28 Thompson (2000), p. 52.
29 See, for example, Bolman and Deal (2001); Boyatzis and McKee (2005); Cooper and Sawaz (1998); Covey (2004); Delbecq (2006); Giacalone and Jurkiewicz (2003); Goleman (1998); Lamont (2002); Lewin and Regine (1999); Zohar and Marshall (2000).
30 Kosmos Journal Spring/Summer 2004 'Spiritual Intelligence: Why it is important'. Available online: http://www.kosmos journal.org/issue/spring-summer-2004?A=SearchResult& SearchID=2544373&ObjectID=3846222&ObjectType=35 (accessed September 2012).
31 Zohar and Marshall (2000), p. 207.
32 Abraham H. Maslow (1969) The Psychology of Science. Chicago, IL: Henry Regnery Company. Here he introduces a further hierarchy: self-transcendence, which he argues sits above self-actualisation.

# Chapter 3

1 See specifically recent guidelines on Promoting Well-Being in the Workplace published in the UK by the National Institute for Clinical Excellence. Available online: http://www.nice.org.uk/ newsroom/nicenewslettersandalerts/intopractice-newsletter forimplementers/niceguidanceandyourworkplace.jsp (accessed 2 August 2011).
2 Frankl (2004), p. 81
3 See Chapter 2.
4 See Chapter 2.
5 Lecture delivered in London, England in December 2009. Author's notes.
6 Conducted in September 2008. There was a North-South divide with 72 per cent of Portuguese finding it difficult compared to 20 per cent of Finns. (UK = 32 per cent). At 55 per cent, women were more likely to find it difficult than men (46 per cent). It is unclear whether the higher incidence is due to greater work demands or to a higher value being placed on family interaction.
7 See, for example, The Work Foundation 's research report for UNISON: 'Work-Life Balance: Rhetoric Versus Reality?' Available online: www.theworkfoundation.com/assets/docs/ publications/155_unison.pdf

8 Cited in the Association for Coaching Newsletter, Oct 2009. Available online: www.associationforcoaching.com (accessed October 2012).
9 For example, MBTI (http://en.wikipedia.org/wiki/MBTI); SIMA (www.sima.co.uk) (accessed October 2012).
10 Covey, ibid.
11 Stanford Report, August 24, 2009, by Adam Gorlick. Available online: http://news.stanford.edu/news/2009/august24/multitask-research-study-082409.html (accessed 16 August 2011).
12 See: http://www.theworkfoundation.com/difference/e4wlb/jargonbuster.aspx#T (accessed October 2012).
13 CIPD – The UK Chartered Institute of Personnel and Development; HSE – Health and Safety Executive.
14 Coaching at Work, Vol. 3 Issue 6, p. 24.
15 Written up in an article dated 24 December 2008 and entitled: 'The Complex Relationship Between Religion and Purpose'. Available online: http://www.gallup.com/poll/113575/complex-relationship-between-religion-purpose.aspx (accessed 2 August 2011).
16 Frankl (2004), p. 85.
17 Ibid., p. 105.
18 There's an important section on 'Energy' later in this chapter.
19 This assumption only goes back perhaps 50 years.
20 See: www.authentichappiness.sas.upenn.edu/Default.aspx (accessed October 2012).
21 Jeffers (2007).
22 For the purposes here, I am assuming that this does not go into realms requiring trained therapy.
23 See, for example, Rob Cross (2009) Grad Expectations: The Essential Guide for All Graduates Entering the Work Force. St Albans: Ecademy Press.
24 The control an individual has over their work and workload, including when, where and how they work. See earlier in this chapter.
25 See, for example, Tony Schwartz and Catherine McCarthy (2007) 'Manage Your Energy, Not Your Time'. Harvard Business Review, October.
26 Ibid.
27 Source: anonymously posted on YouTube.

28  Charles B. Handy (1990) Understanding Voluntary Organisations: How to Make Them Function Effectively. London: Penguin Business.

## Chapter 4

1  This is my version of a classic folk story that seems to exist in several different forms, original source unknown.
2  Commonly triggered by the youngest child leaving home.
3  Wigglesworth and McElhenie (2006), p. 23.
4  This is illustrated at the end of this chapter.
5  I repeat the warning against coaches entering into realms of counselling not within their remit or skill-set.
6  Sourced from the website http://www.ednamurdoch.com/ (accessed December 2009).
7  Ronald L. Grimes (1994) The Beginnings of Ritual Studies. Columbia, SC: University of South Carolina Press.
8  See, for example, Coutu (2002).
9  Viktor Frankl says he survived Auschwitz by imagining himself 'giving a lecture after the war on the psychology of the concentration camp', to help outsiders understand what he had been through. In other words, this is how he found a sense of meaning.
10  Roy A. Rappaport (1999) Ritual and Religion in the Making of Humanity. Cambridge: Cambridge University Press.

## Chapter 5

1  In the UK, these are schools are run by a church denomination (or a non-Christian faith) and funded partly by that group and partly by the state. They are allowed and expected to reflect the ethos of that faith.
2  See, for example, Mintzberg (1989).
3  See, for example, Covey (2004); Coutu (2002); Giacalone and Jurkiewicz (2003); Goleman (1995); Senge (2001); Thompson (2000).
4  Speech delivered at The Stakeholder Engagement Summit 2008, Barcelona, 13–14 October 2008.
5  Griffiths (2009).
6  Written by the author.

7 Quoted in Howard and Welbourn (2004).
8 Senge (2001), p. 551.
9 Janiece Webb, Senior Vice President, Motorola. Quoted on the SHINE website: http://info.shine.com/Career-Advice-Articles/Career-Advice/Can-spirituality-and-business-coexist/2777/cid2.aspx (accessed December 2010).
10 See for example: Boyatzis and McKee (2005); Covey (2004); Delbecq (2006); Giacalone and Jurkiewicz (2003); Howard and Welbourn (2004); Lewin and Regine (1999); Poole (2006); Robinson (2008).
11 For a broader discussion of these issues, see Chapter 2.
12 Small to medium enterprises, commonly defined as less than 250 employees but typically with 1–5.
13 Interview in The Times, 24 January 2009.
14 See for example: Peters and Waterman (1994); Collins and Porras (1994); Lamont (2002).
15 Delbecq (2006).
16 Korac-Kakabadse et al. (2002), p. 168.
17 Quoted in Howard and Welbourn (2004), p. 121.
18 Wigglesworth and McElhenie (2006).
19 Goleman, Boyatzis and McKee (2002).
20 Neuschel (2005), p. 95.

# Chapter 6

1 See Chapter 7 and the bibliography for some examples.
2 Hopson and Scally (2008).
3 According to one MBTI survey, out the 16 types, even the category with the lowest belief in a Higher Spiritual Power (INTJ) has almost 65 per cent support. For those with an F preference, it rises to 90 per cent and above. Briggs Myers et al. (2003), p. 237–8. For those wishing to explore how it is expressed in each preference, see: www.mbtitoday.org/articles/article07.html (accessed October 2012).
4 See additional detail in Chapter 7.
5 More detail is given in Chapter 7.
6 Roberto Assagioli (1975) refers to this as our superconscious.
7 See Chapter 7.
8 Research Professor at Emory University in Atlanta, Georgia.
9 Fowler's stages are covered in Chapter 7.

10 Westerhoff (2000) and briefly outlined in Chapter 7.
11 Where the core abilities are present but not the specifics, that might be the realm of the mentor, typically someone fully experienced in the industry and skills of the recipient.
12 Birch (2001), p. 17.
13 Whitworth (2007), pp. 7–13.
14 Developed by Peter Hawkins: see http://www.personal-coaching-information.com/clear-coaching-model.html (accessed October 2012).
15 Wilson (2007), pp. 42–47.
16 Passmore (2006).
17 That is, terms that simply give a hint that something more may be going on below the surface, as opposed to core terminology, that spells it out (e.g. 'Higher Power', 'In my soul', etc.).
18 Myers Briggs Type Indicator: http://www.myersbriggs.org/my-mbti-personality-type/mbti-basics (accessed October 2012).
19 See: www.sima.co.uk (accessed October 2012).
20 See Chapter 7 and the bibliography.
21 Discretionary effort is what we choose to invest in a task (at work or at home) over and above what is obligatory.
22 The Johari Window model is explained in Chapter 7
23 See Chapter 7.
24 www.linkedin.com (accessed October 2012).

## Chapter 7

1 Wigglesworth and McElhenie (2006). Based on research with several thousand workshop and consultation participants.
2 Goleman and Boyatzis: Emotional Intelligence; Goleman (2006) Working with Emotional Intelligence; and Goleman's (1998) Harvard Business Review article, 'What Makes a Leader?'
3 Marjolein Lips-Wiersmahas also developed a four-quadrant model to enable organisations to conduct an audit of SQ awareness. Her Holistic Development Model uses axes of self/other and being/doing. (2003) Making Conscious Choices in Doing Research on Workplace Spirituality. Journal of Organisational Change Management 16(4), pp. 406–425.
4 See: www.consciouspursuits.com (accessed October 2012).
5 Neuschel (2005), p. 95.
6 George Bernard Shaw (1906).

7 Kohlberg (1976).
8 In essence: 'Do to others as you would like them to do to you'.
9 Professor of Developmental Psychology, Candler School of Theology, Atlanta.
10 Fowler (1981).
11 Westerhoff (2000).
12 Spiral Dynamics (and Transpersonal thinking) links with the Integration work of Ken Wilber – see the bibliography).
13 Websites: www.spiraldynamics.com or www.enlightennext.org/magazine/spiral/?ifr=hp-thm (accessed October 2012). Books: Beck and Cowan (2005) Spiral Dynamics: Mastering Values, Leadership and Change. Graves himself has few publications; the most useful source for his work is: Cowan and Todorovic (2005) The Never Ending Quest: Clare W Graves Explores Human Nature. There is an excellent summary and examples of application in Owen (2004) More Magic of Metaphor: Stories for Leaders, Influencers and Motivators.
14 Silsbee (2004).
15 Martsolf and Mickley (1998).

# Bibliography

Assagioli, Roberto (1975) *The Resolution of Conflicts*. New York: Psychosynthesis Research Foundation.

Barber, J. (2005) *Good Question! The art of asking questions to bring about positive change*. Great Yarmouth: Bookshaker.

Beck, D. E. and Cowan, C. (2005) *Spiral Dynamics: Mastering values, leadership and change*. Oxford: Blackwell.

Birch, P. (2001) *Instant Coaching: Inspire others to reach their potential now*. London: Kogan Page.

Bolles, R. N. (1970). *What Color is your Parachute?* Berkeley, CA: Ten Speed Press.

Bolman, L. G. and Deal, T. E. (2001) *Leading with Soul: An uncommon journey of spirit*. San Francisco, CA: Jossey-Bass.

Boyatzis, R. and McKee, A. (2005) *Resonant Leadership: Renewing yourself and connecting with others*. Boston, MA: Harvard Business School Press.

Briggs Myers, I., McCaulley, M. H., Quenk, N. L. and Hammer, A. H. (2003) *MBTI Manual: A guide to the development and use of the MBTI*. Palo Alto: CPP.

Collins, J. C. and Porras, J. I. (1994) *Built to Last*. New York: Harper Business.

Cooper, R. and Sawaz, A. (1998) *Executive EQ: Emotional intelligence in business*. London: Texere Publishing.

Coutu, Diane L. (2002) 'How Resilience Works'. *Harvard Business Review*. May.

Covey, S. R. (2004) *The 8th Habit: From effectiveness to greatness*. New York: Free Press.

Cowan, C. and Todorovic, N. (2005) *The Never Ending Quest: Clare W. Graves explores human nature*. Santa Barbara, CA: ECLET.

His Holiness, the Dalai Lama (2008) *How to See Yourself as You Really Are: A practical guide to self-knowledge*. London: Rider.

Delbecq, A. L. (2006) 'How a Core Spiritual Discipline is Expressed in the Life of Contemporary Organizational Leaders'. *Spirit in Work*, Issue 6 March. Available online: http://www.modem-uk.org/resources/SiW_6.pdf (Accessed October 2012).

Duniho, T. (1991) *Wholeness Lies Within: Sixteen natural paths towards spirituality*. Gladwyne, PA: Type & Temperament (MBTI).

Fowler, J. W. (1981) *Stages of Faith: The psychology of human development and the quest for meaning*. San Francisco, CA: Harper & Row.

Frankl, V. E. (2004) *Man's Search for Meaning*. London: Ebury.

Frost, R. (1916) 'The Road Not Taken'. In *Mountain Interval*. New York: Holt and company.

Giacalone, R. and Jurkiewicz, C. L. (eds) (2003) *Handbook of Workplace Spirituality and Organizational Performance*. New York: ME Sharpe.

Goleman, D. (1995) *Emotional Intelligence: Why it can matter more than IQ*. New York: Bantam Dell (Random).

Goleman, D. (1998) 'What Makes a Leader?' In *Harvard Business Review on What Makes a Leader*. Boston, MA: Harvard Business School Press.

Goleman, D. (2006) *Working with Emotional Intelligence*. New York: Bantam Books.

Goleman, D., Boyatzis, R. and McKee, A. (2002) *Primal Leadership: Realizing the power of emotional intelligence*. Boston, MA: Harvard Business School Press.

Grant, W. H. (1983) *From Image to Likeness: A Jungian path in the Gospel journey*. New York: Paulist Press.

Griffiths, Lord of Fforestfach, former Head of the Prime Minister's Policy Unit (1985–1990) ; at the time of writing, Chair of the Economics Affairs Select Committee in the House of Lords (2009) writing in *The Times*, Thursday 9 April 2009.

Herzberg, F. (1968) 'One More Time: How do you motivate employees?', *Harvard Business Review*, vol. 46, iss. 1, pp. 53–62.

Hoffman, E. (2009) *Time*. London: Profile.

Hopson, B. and Scally, M. (2008). *The Rainbow Years*. London: Middlesex University Publishing.

Howard, S. and Welbourn, D. (2004). *The Spirit at Work Phenomenon*. London: Azure.

Hughes, G. W. (1988) *God of Surprises*. London: Darton, Longman & Todd.

Investors in People Guide (2003) Work-Life Balance. Available online: http://www.investorsinpeople.co.uk (Accessed October 2012).

Jeffers, Susan (2007) *Feel The Fear And Do It Anyway*. London: Vermilion.

Kline, N. (1999) *Time to Think*. London: Ward Lock.

Knight, Sue (2003) *NLP at Work: The difference that makes the difference in business*. London: Nicholas Brealey.

Kohlberg, L. (1976) 'Moral stages and moralization: The cognitive-developmental approach'. In T. Lickona (ed.) *Moral Development and Behavior: Theory, research and social issues*. New York: Holt, Rinehart and Winston.

Korac-Kakabadse, N., Kouzmin, A. and Kakabdase, A. (2002) 'Spirituality and Leadership Praxis'. *Journal of Managerial Psychology*, 17(3), pp. 165–182.

Kratz, A. and Kratz, D., with Art James Productions (1995) *Effective Listening Skills* (Business Express Series). Columbus, OH: McGraw-Hill.

Lajoie, D. H. and Shapiro, S. I. (1992) 'Definitions of Transpersonal Psychology: The first twenty-three years'. *Journal of Transpersonal Psychology* 24(1), pp. 79–98.

Lamont, G. (2002) *The Spirited Business: Success stories of soul-friendly businesses*. London: Hodder & Stoughton.

Lewin, R. and Regine, B. (1999) *The Soul at Work: Unleashing the power of complexity science for business success*. London: Orion Business.

Lips-Wiersma, M. (2003) 'Making Conscious Choices in Doing Research on Workplace Spirituality'. *Journal of Organisational Change Management* 16(4), pp. 406–425.

McCartney, Claire and Holby, Linda (2003) *The Management Report*. Horsham, West Sussex: Roffey Park Institute.

McTaggart, L. (2003) *The Field: The quest for the scientific force of the universe*. London: Element-HarperCollins.Martsolf, D. S. and Mickley J. R. (1998) 'The Concept of Spirituality in Nursing Theories: Differing world-views and extent of focus'. *Journal of Advanced Nursing* 27, pp. 294–303.

Mintzberg, Henry (1989) *Mintzberg on Management: Inside our strange world of organizations*. New York: The Free Press.

Morgan, G. (1997) *Images of Organization*. London: Sage.

Neck, C. P. and Milliman, J. F. (1994) 'Thought Self-Leadership: Finding spiritual fulfilment in organizational life'. *Journal of Managerial Psychology*, 9(6), pp. 9–16.

Neuschel, R. P. (2005) *The Servant Leader: Unleashing the power of your people*. London: Kogan Page/Kellog School of Management.

Nichols, M. P. (2009) *The Lost Art of Listening*. New York: The Guilford Press.

O'Connor, J. and Lages, A. (2004) *Coaching with NLP: How to be a master coach*. London: Element-HarperCollins.

Owen, N. (2001) *The Magic of Metaphor*. Carmarthen: Crown House.

Owen, N. (2004) *More Magic of Metaphor: Stories for leaders, influencers and motivators*. Carmarthen: Crown House.

Palmer, P. J. (2000) *Let Your Life Speak: Listening for the voice of vocation*. San Francisco, CA: Jossey-Bass.

Palmer, S. (2007) *Transpersonal Psychology Redux: Purpose, meaning and stages of consciousness*. Paper presented to the 3rd Annual Conference of The British Psychological Society.

Parsons, R. (1999) *The Sixty Minute Father*. London: Hodder & Stoughton.

Passmore, J. (ed.) (2006) *Excellence in Coaching: The industry guide*. London: Kogan Page.

Peters, T. J. and Waterman, R. H. (1994) *In Search of Excellence*. New York: Harper & Row.

Plato. *The Republic Book VII*. In R. A. H. Waterfield (trans.) (1993) Oxford: Oxford University Press.

Poole, E. (2006) *Organisational Spirituality*. Ashridge Business School. Available online: http://www.ashridge.org.uk/Website/IC.nsf/wFARATT/Organisationalpercent20Spiritualitypercent20-percent20Awaypercent20withpercent20thepercent20Fairiespercent20-percent202006/$file/OrganisationalSpirituality-AwayWithTheFairies.pdf (Accessed December 2010).

Richardson, P. T. (1996) *Four Spiritualities: A psychology of spiritual choice*. Palo Alto, California: Davies-Black Publishing.

Riddell, M. (2000) *Sacred Journey*. Oxford: Lion.

Robinson, P. (2008) *Spirituality and the City*. London: The London Centre for Spirituality. Available online: http://www.spirituality

centre.org/export/sites/default/resourcesandlinks/presentation_03.ppt (Accessed October 2012).

Senge, P. (1994) *The 5th Discipline: Strategies and tools for building a learning organization*. London: Nicholas Brealey.

Senge, P. (2001) *Dance of Change: The challenges of sustaining momentum in learning organizations*. London: Nicholas Brealey.

Shaw, Bernard (1906) *Dramatic Opinions and Essays*. New York: Brentano's.

Silsbee, D. K. (2004) *The Mindful Coach*. Marshall, NC: Ivy River Press.

Starr, J. (2008) *The Coaching Manual: The definitive guide to the process, principles and skills of personal coaching*. London: Pearson/Prentice Hall Business.

Strauss, William and Howe, Neil (1991) *Generations: The history of America's future, 1584 to 2069*. New York: Quill William Morrow.

Thompson, C. M. (2000) *The Congruent Life: Following the inward path to fulfilling work and inspired leadership*. San Francisco, CA: Jossey-Bass.

Tolle, E. (2005) *The Power of Now: A guide to spiritual enlightenment*. London: Hodder & Stoughton.

Vaill, P. B. (1998) *Spirited Leading and Learning: Process wisdom for a new age*. San Francisco, CA: Jossey-Bass.

Watkins, J. M. and Mohr, B. J. (2001) *Appreciative Inquiry: Change at the speed of imagination*. San Francisco, CA: Jossey-Bass.

Westerhoff, J., III (2000) *Will Our Children Have Faith?* New York: Seabury.

Whitmore, J. (2004) *Coaching for Performance: GROWing people, performance and purpose*. London: Nicholas Brealey.

Whitworth, L., Kimsey-House, K., Kimsey-House, H. and Sandahl, P. (2007) *Co-active Coaching: New skills for coaching people towards success in work and life*. Mountain View, CA: Davies-Black.

Whyte, D. (2002) *The Heart Aroused: Poetry and the preservation of the soul in corporate America*. New York: Doubleday.

Wigglesworth, C. (2004) 'Spiritual Intelligence: Why it matters'. *Kosmos Journal* spring/summer. Available online: http://www.kosmosjournal.org/issue/spring-summer-2004?A=Search Result&SearchID=2544373&ObjectID=3846222&ObjectType=35 (accessed September 2012).

Wigglesworth, C. and McElhenie, M. (2006) *Validation Study for a Measure of Spiritual Intelligence*. Bellaire, TX: Conscious Pursuits Ltd.

Wilber, K. (2000) *A Theory of Everything: An integral vision for business, politics, science and spirituality*. Boston, MA: Shambala Publications.

Wilson, C. (2007) *Best Practice in Performance Coaching: A handbook for leaders, coaches, HR professionals and organizations*. London: Kogan Page.

Zohar, D. and Marshall, I. (2000) *Spiritual Intelligence, the Ultimate Intelligence?* London: Bloomsbury.

Zohar, D. and Marshall, I. (2004) *Spiritual Capital: Wealth we can live by*. London: Bloomsbury.

# Index

absenteeism 53, 54
acceptance of reality 95
accreditation, professional 174
achiever (Orange) 192
actions 19–20
active listening 164–5
Adams, D. 24
ADAPT model 158
affiliative faith 187
age-related change 10
alchemist/magician (Turquoise) 192
alchemy 94–8
Argyris, C. 18
Assagioli, R. 27
Association for Spirit at Work 197
attitudes 19–20, 25
authority and social order-maintaining orientation 183, 184, 189

baby-boomers 10, 21, 57
baggage 84–5
Balanced Life 53–60, 154; *see also* work-life balance
basic survival needs 25

Beck, D. 188, 193
becoming 195; *see also* Existential Leap
Beige 147, 190, 193
beliefs 19–20, 22–3, 95–6, 195; self-limiting 45
belonging, social 25, 26
Blue 147, 190, 192, 194
body 56–7
body language 164
Bolles, R.N. 16
Boyatzis, R. 20, 178
business (executive) coaching 8, 54
business organisations 101–38; overcoming barriers 115–28; value of spirituality to 109–15; workplace context and spirituality 102–15

Campbell, J. 62, 88
cave allegory 17
Center for Visionary Leadership 197
challenge 123
Chopra, D. 80
CLEAR model 159
closed questions 166

coaching: defining 7–8, 152–4; development of and the search for meaning 8–9
coaching models 155–9; *see also* GROW model
coaching skills 141–76; identifying characteristics of good coaching 154–5; language skills 159–64; listening skills 164–5; professional practice 172–5; questioning skills 165–72, 175–6, 181–2; stages of life and faith 147–51; understanding oneself and others 145–7
CO-ACTIVE model 158–9
competencies 132–3, 178–9
concentration camps 61, 207
Conger, J. 41
connectivity 4, 41, 97, 110, 195; value of 113–15
contemplation 130
contextual change 15, 16–23
continuing professional development 174
conventional level of moral reasoning 183, 184, 189
core terminology 7
core values 20–1, 22, 96–7, 135
corporate social responsibility 66, 104, 112
corridors and rooms 43–5, 161
counselling 12, 85–6
Coutu, D.L. 95–6
Covey, S. 53, 56
Cowan, C. 188, 191, 193
creativity 6

crises 10, 61–2, 83–99, 108; coach as alchemist 94–8; coaching implications 88–94; culturally specific 87; economic crisis 16, 105–6, 108–9; life-cycle 87–8; mid-life crisis 62–3, 70, 88, 94–5; rituals 98–9; universal 86–7
cultural audits 102–3
culturally specific crises 87

Dante 72, 84
Delbecq, A. 130
disorientation 44
dissatisfaction-reducers 25
diversity 136–7
divine–human relationship 39
Donne, J. 4

economic crisis 16, 105–6, 108–9
economic value of spirituality 111–13
ego self/higher self-awareness 132, 178
ego self/higher self mastery 132, 133, 178
Elder phase 36, 56, 160
emotional intelligence (EQ) 42–3, 129, 178
emotions 19–20
energy 73–5; levels in crises 89, 91
engagement 23–4
ethics 43, 195; business ethics 115–16, 117; moral development 182–5, 189
EXACT model 159
executive (business) coaching 8, 54

Existential Leap 35–7, 62–3, 88–90, 132, 160–1; life stages and 56, 57; spirituality and work-life balance 67, 69–71, 72
experienced faith 187
expert (Blue) 192
exploration 92

facilitating 153
failure, fear of 173
faith development 66, 147–51, 185–8, 189
family 58
fear of failure 173
fear and obedience orientation 183, 183–4, 189
Fenton, T. 115
'5 Whys' technique 166–7
Foundation for Workplace Spirituality 198, 199
Fowler, J. 148–9, 186–7, 189
Frankl, V. 8, 24, 52, 61, 97, 207
Freud, S. 20, 24, 148

gateway language 6–7, 46–7, 89, 137–8, 161, 180–1
Generation X 10, 57, 66, 143
Generation Y 10, 21, 66, 143
generations 10, 21, 55–8
global interconnectedness 113
goals 64, 88; GROW model 155, 156, 158, 170; noble 18, 18–20, 53; SMART 156
Goleman, D. 20, 128–9, 178
Good Life 65
Graves, C.W. 188, 191, 192, 193
Green 147, 191, 192, 194
group coaching 144

GROW model 69, 92, 155–8; effective questions based on 169–72

Hamel, G. 18
Handy, C. 80, 195
happiness 23–4, 63–4
Haughey, J. 25
heart 56–7
Herzberg, F. 25, 38
hierarchy of needs 25, 26, 46
hindsight in advance technique 79–80
*Hitchhiker's Guide to the Galaxy, The* (Adams) 26
Holby, L. 16
Hopson, B. 76, 144
Hughes, G. 18
human–divine relationship 39
Huxley, A. 148
hypothetical questions 166

Ignatius of Loyola 5–6
illuminator role 164
imperfection, tolerance of 130
improvisation 95
impulsiveness (Purple) 193
individualist (Green) 192
Ingham, H. 195
Institute for Management Excellence 198
institutions 8, 106
interconnectivity *see* connectivity
interest in spirituality 107
International Association for Spiritual Coaching 198
International Center for Spirit at Work 199

interpersonal accord and conformity 183, 184, 189
intuitive-projective faith 186, 189

James, W. 26
Jeffers, S. 66
job market entrants 57–8, 65–6
Johari window 168–9, 195–7
*Journal of Transpersonal Psychology* 26
Jung, C. 20, 26, 201

King, U. 41
Kline, N. 153
Kohlberg, L. 148, 182–5, 189
Korac-Kakabadse, N. 130

Lajoie, D.H. 26
language 6–7, 62; core 7; gateway 6–7, 46–7, 89, 137–8, 161, 180–1
language skills, coaches' 159–64
leadership: servant 130–1; spiritually intelligent 128–34, 179–80, 193
learning: from the past 134; transformative 18
Levinson, D. 189
Life Balance Wheel 77
life coaching 8, 54
life-cycle crises 87–8
life stages 55–8, 147–51, 189
Lips-Wiersmahas, M. 209
listening skills 164–5
Luft, J. 195

'Management's Grand Challenges' 17–18
Marshall, I. 43
Martsolf, D.S. 194–5
Maslow, A. 20, 24, 25, 26, 26–7, 46
materialism 9
McCartney, C. 16
McLaughlin, C. 197–8
meaning 42, 46, 195; Balanced Life 51, 60–6; search for 3–4, 8–14, 40–1; and sense-making 15, 23–37
meaning-based language 62
*Meaning of Life, The* 26
Meaningful Life 65
memes 188
mentoring 7–8, 153
Mezirow, J. 18
Mickley, J.R. 194–5
mid-life crisis 62–3, 70, 88, 94–5; *see also* Existential Leap
Milliman, J.F. 109
mind 56–7
mindfulness 194–7
Mintzberg, H. 18
moral development 182–5, 189
Morgan, G. 111
motivation 80, 81, 154
multiple intelligences 91, 128–9, 177–8; *see also* emotional intelligence (EQ), spiritual intelligence (SQ)
multitasking 59
Myers Briggs Type Indicator (MBTI) 147, 163
Myners, Lord 112
mythic entrancement 16–18, 53
mythic-literal faith 186, 189

National Institute for Clinical Excellence 53

INDEX 221

Neck, C.P. 109
needs, hierarchy of 25, 26, 46
noble goals 18, 18–20, 53
Nohari window 197
non-listening organisation 12, 145–6

open questions 166
opportunisms (Red) 193
Orange 147, 190–1, 192, 194
organisational culture 110–11
owned faith 188

peace, radiating 131
performance bonuses 105–6, 111
personality 55–8
personality profiling questionnaires 163
personality types 146–7, 208
Plato 17
Pleasant Life 65
pleasure 23
Poole, E. 109
post-conventional level of moral reasoning 183, 184–5, 189
potential 123, 152
pre-conventional level of moral reasoning 183, 183–4, 189
presenteeism 53
probing questions 166
professional accreditation 174
professional bodies 198–9
professional development, continuing 174
professional practice 172–5
Purchase, R. 70–1
Purple 147, 190, 193, 194
purpose 123

questioning skills 165–72, 175–6, 181–2

rapport 175
reality: acceptance of 95; GROW model 92, 155, 156, 156–7, 170–1
Red 147, 190, 193
referral 85–6, 90
reflective questions 166
relative values 20
religion: faith development 66, 147–51, 185–8, 189; spirituality and 6, 23, 44, 159–60, 169–70
reorientation 43–4
resilience 95–7
rituals 98–9
Robinson, P. 110
role models 98
rooms and corridors 43–5, 161
Rumi 135

safety and security needs 25
satisfaction 63–4
satisfaction-builders 25, 26
Scally, M. 76, 144
scientific management 103–4
searching faith 187–8
security and safety needs 25
self-actualisation need 25, 39
self-awareness 132, 178
self-esteem need 25, 26
self-interest orientation 183, 184, 189
self-limiting beliefs 45
self mastery 132, 133, 151, 178
self-serving manager 12, 145–6, 149–51
self-understanding 145–7

Seligman, M. 23, 65
Senge, P. 18, 20, 107–8
sense-making 15, 23–37
servant leadership 130–1
Shakespeare, W. 9
Shapiro, S. 26, 64
Shaw, G.B. 3, 182
signature strengths 65–6
signpost events 72
signpost questions 71–2
silence 166, 172–3
SMART goals 156
social belonging 25, 26
social contract orientation 183, 184–5, 189
social mastery/spiritual presence 132, 133, 178
Solzhenitsyn, A. 97
soul (spirit) 56–7, 74, 135–6
space 130
Spiral Dynamics 147, 188–94; Tier 1 190–1; Tier 2 191–2, 193
spirit (soul) 56–7, 74, 135–6
spirit-based language 62
spiritual intelligence (SQ) 11, 42–3, 61, 66, 111, 144, 151; and the Balanced Life 72–3; development of 41, 72–3, 177–9; measuring 131–3; need for 107–8; Spiral Dynamics 188–94
spiritual presence/social mastery 132, 133, 178
spirituality 3, 6, 11–12, 15, 37–45, 46, 61, 201–2; adding real value 13–14; coaching questions 181–2; functions of 40; religion and 6, 23, 44, 159–60, 169–70; as specialism in coaching 143–52; work-life balance 51, 66–75
spiritually intelligent leadership 128–34; characteristics 128–33; common traits 179–80; Tier 2 leaders 193
stages of development 91; faith development 147–51, 186–8, 189; life stages 55–8, 147–51, 189; moral development 182–5, 189; Spiral Dynamics 147, 188–94; spiritual development 41, 72–3, 177–9; spiritually intelligent leaders 131–3
standards 195
strategist (Yellow) 192
stress 60
supervision 174, 199
'sweet spot' activities 74
synthetic-conventional faith 186–7, 189
System for Identifying Motivated Abilities (SIMA) 163–4

Taylor, F.W. 103–4
terminology *see* language
Thompson, C.M. 9
time 130
time management 58–60
time sovereignty 59–60
tolerance of imperfection 130
training 198
transcendence 38, 195
transcendental morality 185
transformative learning 18
transition 44

transpersonal dimension 11, 26–7
Turquoise 147, 191–2, 192

universal awareness 132–3, 151, 178
universal crises 86–7
universal ethical principles 183, 185, 189

value: proposition 117; of spirituality to an organisation 109–15
values 19–20, 20–2, 95–6, 195; core 20–1, 22, 96–7, 135; relative 20
values-based language 62
voice 164

Warrior phase 36, 56, 160
Webb, J. 109–10
well-being 63–4

Westerhoff, J. 149, 187–8
Whitmore, J. 11, 27, 155
Wigglesworth, C. 23, 43, 88, 129, 131–3, 151, 178, 179
will 155, 156, 157–8, 172
Williams, G. 114
work-life balance 21, 51–82; activities to provide insight 76–82; expression of spirituality 51, 66–75; search for meaning 51, 60–6
workplace: context and spirituality 102–15; opportunities to explore spirituality 151–2
WorldBlu 115
worldview 194

Yellow 147, 191, 192

Zedelius, W. 105
Zohar, D. 43